Acclaim for
'You Did It to M~~e~~'

It is clear that the power of th
moved Fr. Gaitley to write this bo
compassion put into action.

Today, so many people are de   ......u by the cruelty
and indifference of the culture around us. We Christians are
called through our faith, our prayers, and our deeds to become
the living presence of Christ's mercy in our world.

As a prison chaplain who works on the largest death row
in the Western hemisphere, I am grateful to Fr. Gaitley for
remembering those in prison, those who our society treats
as the "least of our brothers and sisters." It is through the
prisoners I have known that I have seen the face of Jesus shine
forth. I hope many who read this book will be moved to serve
him by caring for and visiting those in prison.

— **FR. GEORGE WILLIAMS, SJ**
Catholic Chaplain, San Quentin State Prison

Saint Francis of Assisi attributed his conversion to his encounters with the lepers outside the city of Assisi. By extending
mercy to others, Francis came to know and accept the full
magnitude of the mercy that God poured out upon him.

In his new book, *'You Did It to Me,'* Fr. Michael Gaitley,
MIC, provides the tools to assist each one of us in being merciful in our daily lives. Father Gaitley uses extensive examples
from his own life to open our eyes and our hearts to the many
ways we can be more loving and merciful. Of particular help are
the "Action Items" he provides for putting mercy into action.

Father Gaitley's book will not only help us become more
merciful, it will help us come to know and accept God's mercy
in our own lives as well.

— **FR. SEAN SHERIDAN, TOR**
President, Franciscan University of Steubenville

Once we admit how much we stand in need of the mercy of God and receive that mercy for our sins, we are in a position to understand more how much God desires to use us as vessels of his mercy for others. Father Gaitley's book *You Did It to Me* shows us how to extend the mercy we have received. The spiritual wisdom and inspiration in this book will lead the reader into a much deeper understanding of the Heart of God. Its workbook style will help us to apply the teaching concretely and, let's hope, make us fruitful stewards of the mercy that flows from the Heart of God. I highly recommend it!

— SR. ANN SHIELDS, SGL
Renewal Ministries, Ann Arbor, Michigan

Father Michael Gaitley has a gift for communicating Divine Mercy in such a compelling manner, lovingly nudging us closer to Christ and helping to guide our pilgrim's journey toward holiness. I strongly encourage you to read this book!

— TOM PETERSON
President and Founder, Catholics Come Home

Father Gaitley has embraced the task of discussing how we who are Christians are called to live the corporal and spiritual works of mercy. His approach is thought-provoking, challenging, and clear. He handles the material with joy and humor while providing a blue-print for practical action. This is a book that stays in your mind. You will be changed by it!

— VICTORIA THORN
Founder, Project Rachel

I have had the privilege of editing all of Fr. Gaitley's books for Marian Press, and while I love every one of them, this one really blew me away. I believe it will become a spiritual classic, right up there with *33 Days to Morning Glory*.

— DAVID CAME
Executive Editor, Marian Press

'You Did It to Me'

A Practical Guide to Mercy in Action

Fr. Michael E. Gaitley, MIC

MARIAN PRESS
STOCKBRIDGE MA 01263

2016

Available from:
Marian Helpers Center
Stockbridge, MA 01263

Prayerline:1-800-804-3823
Orderline: 1-800-462-7426
Website: TheDivineMercy.org

ISBN: 978-1-59614-304-3
First edition (3rd printing): 2016

Cover Art: Michelangelo's "Last Judgment," Sistine Chapel

Page Design: Curtis Bohner

Editing and Proofreading: David Came, Sarah Chichester,
Chris Sparks, and Andy Leeco

Imprimi Potest:
Very Rev. Kazimierz Chwalek, MIC
Provincial Superior
The Blessed Virgin Mary, Mother of Mercy Province
Congregation of Marian Fathers of the Immaculate Conception
March 3, 2014

For texts from the English Edition of *Diary of St. Maria Faustina Kowalska*

Nihil Obstat:
George H. Pearce, SM
Former Archbishop of Suva, Fiji

Imprimatur:
Joseph F. Maguire
Bishop of Springfield, MA
April 9, 1984

Printed in the United States of America

To St. Faustina

If a soul does not exercise mercy somehow or other, it will not obtain My mercy on the day of judgment. Oh, if only souls knew how to gather eternal treasure for themselves, they would not be judged, for they would forestall My judgment with their mercy.

— Jesus to St. Faustina

Contents

Preface

There are plenty of books on the works of mercy. So why write another one? Good question. Here are my main reasons for writing:

1. *A Hugely Important Topic.* The works of mercy are a matter of life and death — as in *eternal* life and death. If we do not practice them, we will not be saved. (See Mt 25:31-46 and Jas 2:14-17.) So, because this is such an important topic, there's certainly room for another book.

2. *A Major Mercy Saint.* At present, no other book on the works of mercy taps deeply into the wisdom of the great mercy saint of our time, Maria Faustina Kowalska. Her witness to mercy sheds more light on the works of mercy, and this writing makes ample use of her teaching.

3. *Give Me a 'How-To.'* Other books on the works of mercy offer practical suggestions on how to put mercy into action. However, their suggestions often take second place to anecdotes and theological explanations. This makes it way too easy to walk away from the reading without a concrete action plan. But that, in my opinion, is what's most needed. Let's face it: None of us is a Mother Teresa. In other words, all of us can do a better job living the works of mercy. But how? How can we live them daily, concretely, and consistently? This book aims to thoroughly answer these questions.

4. *Give Me Simplicity.* Most approaches to the works of mercy follow the traditional 14-point list. Now, I don't know about you, but for me, a list of 14 things is a bit daunting. Therefore, while this book certainly incorporates all 14 of the corporal and spiritual works of mercy, it's organized around the much simpler structure of the five Scriptural categories. (Five points are obviously easier to handle than 14.) Plus, no other book on the works of mercy has the added bonus of a ninja-fied memory device to make things even simpler. (You'll see.)

5. *THANK YOU, LORD!* I don't mean to blame the Lord for this
book, but I believe he had a hand in it. I say this because,
when I first sat down to write, I sort of made a deal with
him. I prayed, "Alright, Lord, I think you want me to write
this book, and I'll give it a shot, but I don't have a lot of
time. So, you'll really have to blast me with some inspiration here." Well, I think he did, because just one week after
making that prayer, the whole book was done! (You can be
the judge of whether it really was him or just the coffee.)

Alright, so that sums up why I wrote a book on the works
of mercy. I hope you will enjoy it as much as I enjoyed writing
it. Yes, I actually found joy in penning these pages during that
whirlwind of a week. And this seems fitting because, in the end,
joy is really what the works of mercy are all about: the joy of
giving, the joy of receiving, the joy of heaven that comes as a
reward. I pray that this book will help you to experience such
joy even more abundantly.

Before signing off, I'd like to thank my friends who read
this manuscript and offered their insightful comments: Eric
Mahl, Lewis Brooks, Mark Fanders, Ben O'Neill, Chris Sparks,
and especially David Came and Sarah Chichester.

Fr. Michael E. Gaitley, MIC, STL
National Shrine of The Divine Mercy
Stockbridge, Massachusetts
Divine Mercy Sunday
April 27, 2014

PART ONE

Introduction

CHAPTER ONE
'You Did It to Me
... You Did Not Do It to Me'

One day, one great and terrible day, one of these two sentences will be for each of us either heaven or hell. They'll ring in our ears for all eternity either as a blessing or a curse. They'll lead us either to praise, glory, and honor or to horror, regret, and everlasting despair.

This book is about getting the blessing.

What am I talking about? I'm talking about what we read in Matthew 25:31-46, one of the most important passages in all of Sacred Scripture. It's so important because it tells us *exactly* what we can expect at the end of time, which is this: Christ the King, full of majesty and glory, will either say to us, "Come, O blessed of my Father, inherit the kingdom prepared for you from the foundation of the world." Or he will say — God forbid! — "Depart from me, you cursed, into the eternal fire prepared for the devil and his angels."

Michelangelo's "Last Judgment," Sistine Chapel.

Scripture doesn't lie. Heaven and hell are real. And this life is a drama during which we decide where we will end up *forever*. According to the Word of God, this most important decision is based on how we treat others, particularly those in greatest need. To be exact, the Lord will say to the blessed of heaven:

> I was hungry and you gave me food, I was thirsty and you gave me drink, I was a stranger and you welcomed me, I was naked and you clothed me, I was sick and you visited me, I was in prison and you came to me.

These blessed ones will then respond, "Lord, when? When did we see you hungry, thirsty, a stranger, naked, sick, and imprisoned?" And he will say, "Truly, I say to you, as you did it to one of the least of my brethren, *you did it to me*."

To the cursed of hell, the Lord will declare:

> I was hungry and you gave me no food, I was thirsty and you gave me no drink, I was a stranger and you did not welcome me, I was naked and you did not clothe me, sick and in prison and you did not visit me.

These cursed ones will respond, "Lord, when did we see you hungry, thirsty, a stranger, naked, sick, or in prison and did not minister to you?" The Lord will answer, "Truly, I say to you, as you did it not to one of the least of these, *you did not do it to me*."

Now, I have a confession to make. Sometimes when I pick up a book and it cites a long passage from Sacred Scripture, I don't read the passage. I stupidly say, "Oh, I know this one," and then I proceed to skip it. I've got to stop that. And I'm probably not the only one with this problem, which is why I purposely didn't start this section with the full citation from Matthew 25:31-46. Instead, I mixed it in with lots of other paragraphs, so it would be harder to skip.

We definitely do not want to skip these verses. I mean, yes, we've all heard the Last Judgment story many times — but how seriously are we taking it? How well are we living it? Chances are, if you're reading this book, you know you can do better. You know we all need help putting mercy into action.

Mercy? Yes, mercy. That's what the "big test" of this life is really all about. That's what Christ the King of Majesty will be talking about on the last day. His words will confirm the "blessed" as the merciful and the "cursed" as the unmerciful. To get ready for that most important day, the million-dollar question for each one of us is this: Are we people of mercy or not? Or better yet, the billion-dollar question is, "How do we better *become* people of mercy?" After all, when it comes to living mercy, there's always room to improve.

Because everything hinges on mercy — "everything" being our eternal salvation — let's look more closely at what mercy is.

CHAPTER TWO

What Is Mercy?

Mercy is love when it encounters suffering. It's when love meets the poor, weak, and broken — the "least," as Matthew 25:40 puts it. More specifically, mercy is two movements that take place within us when we see someone (or something) suffer. The first is an emotional movement, a movement of compassion that we feel in our hearts or even, when the suffering of the other is particularly intense, deep in our guts. The second is a movement of action. In other words, as we see someone suffering and feel compassion for him, we soon find ourselves reaching out to alleviate his suffering. In sum: Mercy is love that feels compassion for those who suffer (heart) and reaches out to help them (arms).

This book is about the "arms" part of mercy, mercy in action. Therefore, I'm not going to be treating the important question of *how to make your heart more compassionate*. However, if you do want to learn more about it, I've written another book that focuses almost entirely on this process. It's called *Consoling the Heart of Jesus*.[1] Now, before we move on to the works of mercy, I'd like to say more about this particular book, because its central theme touches on something that's especially important for understanding mercy and the works of mercy.

T*HE 'FOUNDATION OF MERCY.'* I wrote *Consoling the Heart of Jesus* during my first semester of theology studies in the seminary, which was pretty crazy. I mean, at that time, I'd never written a book, had no real training as a writer, and was totally swamped with classes and homework. But it didn't matter. There was a fire in my heart that I had to put on paper.

The fire was based on an insight I'd received in prayer, which was this: I can *console* Jesus; I can alleviate the suffering of his Sacred Heart; I can show him mercy! Before this revelation, I thought my relationship with Jesus was just a one-way street, that he only had mercy on me. I can't tell you what it meant to realize that I could also have mercy on him!

Now, people will say, "Of course, you can have mercy on Jesus. You do so by having mercy on your neighbor." And they're right. After all, that's what the passage from Matthew 25 is all about, "*You did it to me.*" For, indeed, when we console our neighbors, we truly are consoling Jesus *in the members of his Mystical Body.* However, we can also console Jesus in another sense. We can console him as "Jesus himself," so to speak, as *the Head of the Body.* That's the remarkable insight that hit me so hard, the insight I wanted to share in *Consoling the Heart of Jesus.* It's also an insight that I'd like to say more about now, because it will shed a lot of light on how we approach our topic.

As I mentioned earlier, mercy is a form of love. Now, the works of mercy that we'll be covering in this book are acts of love *toward our neighbor.* But what is the foundation of love of neighbor? Love of God. Yes, love of God comes first. Well, similarly with *merciful* love. In fact, just as the love of God is the foundation for our love of neighbor, so also the mercy we have on God (in Jesus) is the foundation for the mercy we show our neighbor. Blessed Mother Teresa provides us with a great example of this.

Blessed Teresa started her work with the poor when, one day, she was walking the streets of Calcutta, saw a man dying in the gutter, and her heart welled up with compassion. From that moment on, she knew she was to help the poor in the streets. Right? Wrong. It wasn't that way. Mother Teresa's work began as a call from Jesus on the Cross, who invited her to quench his Sacred Heart's burning thirst for love. Only after entering more deeply into the mystery of his Heart did she also come to recognize a call to quench Jesus' thirst for love in the hearts of the poor and the suffering.[2]

Thus, the Missionaries of Charity, the community Mother Teresa established, begin each day with a Holy Hour, quenching the thirst of Jesus for their love before they go out to the streets and quench his thirst for love in the poorest of the poor. And this is how it should be. The foundation of a life of mercy is centered on having compassion on the thirsting Heart of

Jesus. For, indeed, Jesus' wounded, broken, suffering Heart is the most deserving of our compassion. When we draw close to it, it heals our own hearts, makes them more compassionate, and strengthens us to put our compassion into action. So, again, having mercy on God (in Jesus) is the foundation for showing mercy to our neighbor.

This point of starting with Jesus' Heart is so important. It's what I call the "Foundation of Mercy." And that's why I recommend making the *Consoling the Heart of Jesus* retreat if you haven't already. Or at least let your love for Jesus the Head of the Body, let your compassion for Jesus' Eucharistic and Sacred Heart be the foundation for your works of mercy to the members of his Body. Without this foundation, the works of mercy become mere social work and do-goodery.

Missionaries of Charity and the "Foundation of Mercy."

Mercy from a pedestal is not really mercy.

*N*O *PEDESTALS!* Okay, one last point before we dive into the works of mercy, a point that's hugely important for understanding mercy and the works of mercy: *Mercy cannot be done from a pedestal.* Anytime we bring out the pedestal and shower mercy down on people from above, anytime we see ourselves as mini-messiahs, anytime we think, "How good it is of me to help that poor person," then it is NOT mercy. What? This may sound strange, but it comes from none other than St. Pope John Paul II.

In his famous encyclical letter on mercy, *Dives in Misericordia*, Pope John Paul says that true mercy is always a two-way street, a "bi-lateral" reality, where both the giver and the receiver are blessed. In fact, he teaches that if we don't realize this when we perform a work of mercy, it's not really mercy! See for yourself:

> We must also continually purify all our actions and all our intentions in which mercy is understood and practiced in a unilateral way, as a good done to others. An act of merciful love is only really such when we are deeply convinced at the moment that we perform it that we are at the same time receiving mercy from the people who are accepting it from us. If this bilateral and reciprocal quality is absent, our actions are not yet true acts of mercy, nor has there yet been fully completed in us that conversion to which Christ has shown us the way by His words and example, even to the Cross, nor are we yet sharing fully in the magnificent source of merciful love that has been revealed to us by Him.[3]

Isn't that stunning? So let's put away the pedestals and continually remind ourselves that whenever we help someone, they are also helping us at the same time. In fact, you might even say that the givers get the better deal. Why? Because as Jesus himself said, "It is more blessed to give than to receive" (Acts 20:35) and because, well — *the receivers save us.* I mean this in the sense that they give us the chance to hear Jesus say to us at the end of time, "Come, O blessed of my Father, inherit the kingdom prepared for you from the foundation of the world." They give us the chance, on the last day, to hear those blessed words of the Lord, "You did it to me." They give us the chance to put mercy into action.

CHAPTER THREE

What Are the Works of Mercy?

I count at least three ways of categorizing the different kinds of works of mercy: (1) The Three Degrees of Mercy, (2) The Traditional Approach, and (3) The Scriptural Approach. Let's look at each of these in turn.

*T*HE *THREE DEGREES OF MERCY.* What I'm calling "The Three Degrees of Mercy" comes from the Divine Mercy message and devotion as revealed to St. Faustina Kowalska. Saint Faustina, an important mystic of the 20th century, recounts her experiences with our Merciful Savior in a diary, which is called *Diary of St. Maria Faustina Kowalska: Divine Mercy In My Soul*. In one passage of this work, Jesus himself teaches Faustina "The Three Degrees of Mercy":

> **I am giving you three ways of exercising mercy toward your neighbor: the first — by deed, the second — by word, the third — by prayer. In these three degrees is contained the fullness of mercy, and it is an unquestionable proof of love for Me. By this means a soul glorifies and pays reverence to My mercy.**[4]

The saint herself comments on these three "degrees" in another passage from her diary:

> The first: the act of mercy, of whatever kind. The second: the word of mercy — if I cannot carry out a work of mercy, I will assist by my words. The third: prayer — if I cannot show mercy by deeds, I can always do so by prayer. My prayer reaches out even there where I cannot reach out physically.[5]

In *Consoling the Heart of Jesus*, I give an in-depth treatment of these three degrees. If you'd like to read that treatment, I've reproduced it in Appendix One. For the body of this book, however, we'll be taking a different approach to the works of mercy.

THE TRADITIONAL APPROACH. The second way of categorizing the various works of mercy is what I call "The Traditional Approach." This approach divides the works of mercy into two major categories: spiritual and corporal. Then, it lists seven sub-categories under each of the two main categories:

CORPORAL WORKS OF MERCY	SPIRITUAL WORKS OF MERCY
1. Feed the hungry.	1. Instruct the ignorant.
2. Give drink to the thirsty.	2. Counsel the doubtful.
3. Clothe the naked.	3. Admonish sinners.
4. Shelter the homeless.	4. Bear wrongs patiently.
5. Comfort the sick.	5. Forgive offenses willingly.
6. Visit the imprisoned.	6. Comfort the afflicted.
7. Bury the dead.	7. Pray for the living & the dead.

In the following paragraph, the *Catechism of the Catholic Church* more or less follows this Traditional Approach:

> The works of mercy are charitable actions by which we come to the aid of our neighbor in his spiritual and bodily necessities. Instructing, advising, consoling, comforting are spiritual works of mercy as are forgiving and bearing wrongs patiently. The corporal works of mercy consist especially in feeding the hungry, sheltering the homeless, clothing the naked, visiting the sick and imprisoned, and burying the dead. Among all these, giving alms to the poor is one of the chief witnesses to fraternal charity: it is also a work of justice pleasing to God.[6]

Notice that the *Catechism* makes one significant addition, which it also singles out for praise: almsgiving. It identifies giving alms to the poor as one of the "chief witnesses to fraternal charity" and something "pleasing to God." We'll say more about this later. For now, let's turn our attention to a third way of categorizing the works of mercy, "The Scriptural Approach."

*T*HE *SCRIPTURAL APPROACH.* The Scriptural Approach covers the five categories mentioned in the Gospel of Matthew 25:31-46: (a) I was hungry, and you gave me food; I was thirsty, and you gave me drink; (b) I was a stranger, and you welcomed me; (c) I was naked, and you clothed me; (d) I was sick, and you visited me; (e) I was in prison, and you came to me. (Notice that, like the *Catechism,* I combine the first two, because their meaning is basically the same.)

Now, it should come as no surprise to learn that there's some overlap between the Scriptural and Traditional approaches. After all, Sacred Scripture and Sacred Tradition are organically related. But actually, there's more than just "some overlap." I say that because *all 14* of the corporal and spiritual works of mercy of the Traditional Approach fit neatly within the five categories of the Scriptural Approach, as you can see below ("c" = "corporal" and "s" = "spiritual"):

(1) "I was hungry, and you gave me food;
        I was thirsty, and you gave me drink."

- Feed the hungry (c. 1).
- Give drink to the thirsty (c. 2).

(2) "I was a stranger, and you welcomed me."

- Shelter the homeless (c. 4).
- Bury the dead (c. 7).
- Bear wrongs patiently (s. 4).
- Forgive offenses willingly (s. 5).

(3) "I was naked, and you clothed me."

- Clothe the naked (c. 3).
- Instruct the ignorant (s. 1).
- Counsel the doubtful (s. 2).
- Comfort the afflicted (s. 6).

(4) "I was sick, and you visited me."

- Comfort the sick (c. 5).

(5) "I was in prison, and you came to me."
- Visit the imprisoned (c. 6).
- Admonish sinners (s. 3).
- Pray for the living and the dead (s. 7).*

In this book, we're going to focus on the Scriptural Approach to the works of mercy. We'll do this not only because the Word of God is full of grace and power, but also because I believe such a five-fold approach provides the easiest way for remembering different works of mercy and putting them into practice. Granted, it's easier to remember the Three Degrees of Mercy, but the Three Degrees may not be concrete enough, at least not for the kind of detailed treatment that's the aim of this book. Of course, someone may respond that two lists of seven (the Traditional Approach) are certainly more detailed than three degrees, and that's true. However, I actually find the Traditional Approach a bit too detailed. I mean, personally, I feel a bit overwhelmed when I'm looking at 14 things, even if they are divided into two categories.

So, I suggest that striking a happy balance when learning about the works of mercy comes not from the simplicity of the three degrees and not from a long list of 14 things but rather the middle ground of the five categories of the Scriptural Approach. My opinion is that most people can pretty easily remember five things and carry the heart of their meaning with them. I say "*the heart of their meaning.*" That's really the goal here. I don't expect you to remember every detail of what follows — don't let the list above scare you! Rather, I expect that we can remember five points and the gist of their meaning. If you're worried you won't be able to remember the list of five, maybe this picture and sentence will help you:

---

* By the way, if some of these groupings of the 14 categories don't make sense now, don't worry. They'll make sense later.

High School Ninjas Stab Porcupines.

What does *this* mean? Well, the logic of the sentence is that ninjas who are in high school are still in training and, therefore, sometimes make stupid mistakes, such as trying to stab a porcupine that clearly has quills longer than a ninja's sword. The poor ninjas who do this end up taking a quill in the belly.

Yes, this is strange, which is why it's easy to remember. And it's helpful to memorize because it reminds us of the five categories of the Scriptural Approach:

High	=	**Hungry**, as in "feed the hungry"
School	=	**Stranger**, as in "welcome the stranger"
Ninjas	=	**Naked**, as in "clothe the naked"
Stab	=	**Sick**, as in "comfort the sick"
Porcupines =		**Prison**, as in "visit those in prison"

Okay, so that's not so hard to remember. And the good news is that now you've got your "cheat sheet" for the most important test of life, the great "Mercy Test." Of course, we have to wait until the Last Judgment to find out whether or not we pass or fail, but at least now we can easily remember what's on the test.

Before we dive into the details of the five categories of the Scriptural Approach, I'd first like to make one point about these details.

As I mentioned earlier, the details of this book are not what are most important. What is most important is that we grasp the main ideas regarding each of the five categories. Still, having said that, there's nothing more annoying than finishing a book and not having anything meaningful to say about it or, more importantly, to do about it. I can't tell you how many times I've had conversations like this:

"Oh, I just read an awesome book."
"Oh, yeah, what did you get out of it?"
"Umm, it was awesome! I really liked it!"
"Cool, so what did you learn?"
"It was just really awesome."

After reading this book, my hope is that we'll not only have something meaningful to say but also many things that will be meaningful to do. Put differently, this really is a guide to mercy *in action*. So, to help us put it into action, at the end of each section, I've provided a list of action items with check-off boxes. If there's an action item you may be able to do, then make sure you check off the box next to it. Then, at the end of the book, in the conclusion, you'll review all your checked boxes and put together a strategy regarding which action items you're going to pursue. Sound good? Alright, then, let's get started.

You May Also Like...

> *For further help putting mercy into action, visit our website, which offers links to numerous charitable organizations, articles, videos, and more.*

 MercyPages.org
It's like the Yellow Pages®
for Works of Mercy!

PART TWO

The Five Scriptural Works
of Mercy Explained

'I Was Hungry and You Gave Me Food;
I Was Thirsty and You Gave Me Drink'

*F*OUR PREFATORY POINTS. As we begin Part Two and before we dive into the topic of this first chapter, I'd like to make four brief points, so you'll know what to expect.

First, in what follows, I'll be offering my own personal interpretation of the five Scriptural works of mercy. Because it's just a personal interpretation, you certainly don't have to agree with me on every point, though I do hope you will find it helpful.

Second, while the chapters of Part Two cover the five categories of the Scriptural Approach, within the chapters, I will identify and explain the 14 works of mercy of the Traditional Approach as they come up. (So, basically, I'm combining the two approaches.)

Third, at the end of each chapter, I will offer several action items to help you put mercy into action.

Fourth, as we read the chapters of Part Two, you'll notice that I don't say much about *almsgiving*. At first, this may seem strange because almsgiving is such an important work of mercy. Not only does the *Catechism* single it out for special praise, as we read earlier, but almsgiving itself relates to every work of mercy we'll be covering. Well, it's precisely for these reasons that I've decided to give almsgiving its own chapter, which follows the chapters on the five Scriptural categories.

*F*EED THE HUNGRY; GIVE DRINK TO THE THIRSTY. This first Scriptural category involves only the corporal works of mercy. Most of the other categories include both corporal *and* spiritual. Here, though, it's all flesh and blood, bread and water.

It's fitting that we start with a purely corporal category because, generally speaking, we should take care of the bodily needs of our neighbor before attending to his spiritual needs. For example, if someone is starving and all we do is preach to him, he will not (and should not) listen to us. Also, the fact that we begin with the corporal works of mercy helps us not to dismiss their importance. And we may need that help. I say this because people can easily fall into the temptation of thinking that what really counts are the spiritual works of mercy. After all, they're... well... *spiritual*, and the spiritual is always better, right? Wrong. What St. Paul refers to as "the flesh" (as in "the spirit vs. the flesh") is evil, but the body itself is good. In fact, as far as the works of mercy are concerned, the corporal and spiritual works are more or less equal. Moreover, this first category, which emphasizes the corporal, reminds us not to excuse ourselves from rolling up our sleeves and doing the often hard and humble work of the corporal works of mercy.

Alright, so we roll up our sleeves and then what? Well, there are many ways to satisfy the hunger and thirst of our neighbor. Most cities and towns have food pantries and soup kitchens that welcome volunteers. (A soup kitchen provides meals for the poor and homeless. A food pantry collects donated food, such as through a can drive, to help families and individuals who live near the poverty line.) Volunteering from time to time or even regularly at a soup kitchen, organizing a food drive, or helping to start a food pantry at your parish are all effective ways of feeding the hungry and giving drink to the thirsty.

Here's another suggestion: Make dinner for a family in need. One of the things my sister most appreciates is when neighbors and friends have made dinner for her family while she was in the hospital — usually after delivering one of her babies. Well, every one of us has probably gone through a trial where we were so sick, suffering, or stressed out that we haven't been able to prepare a meal for ourselves, let alone for anyone else. Making a meal for someone or for a family in such a situation is a great work of mercy. As my sister says, "The greatest thing you can do for a mom is to make a meal for her family!" She was kind of joking, but not really. It is a great thing.

This gets me thinking that homemakers like my sister who cook for their families are themselves putting mercy into action by giving food to the hungry and drink to the thirsty. They may not realize they're doing a work of mercy, but they are, and it's important that they recognize it. So many of our actions can be transformed from what seem like meaningless labor into works of love — *if we consciously choose to make them so.* In other words, every day, each one of us has a choice: Will I do my work mindlessly and grudgingly, or will I do it out of love?

I remember that my mom chose the latter. When I was growing up, my family would sit down for a meal, and as she was putting the food on the table, Mom would often say, "You know, it's got my secret ingredient: *love.*" My brother and I would roll our eyes and tease her for making such a corny statement, but she was actually doing it right. Love really is the "secret ingredient" that transforms our mundane actions into everlasting gifts of glory.

Now, as for the "breadwinners" of the family, those who "bring home the bacon," well, as those phrases aptly imply, they also are feeding the hungry (and giving drink to the thirsty). Going to work every day and earning the wages that buy the food for your family is an act of mercy. I remember coming to realize this truth one day when I went to work with my dad.

From the time I was a little kid, my dad drove a cement truck, helping to build "half of Los Angeles." Well, shortly before his retirement, when I was on break from college, I asked him if I could ride along with him in his cab. He seemed happily surprised by my request, checked with his boss, and gave me the "thumbs up." So, the next day, we got up at 2:15 in the morning, drove to work, hauled the cement, worked on the jobs, and continually cleaned the truck. In the midst of it all, a new appreciation for my dad suddenly dawned on me.

At one point, as we were bouncing around on a hot, smog-filled freeway with a full load of cement, I remember telling my dad, "Dad, you know, every cell in my body exists because you've worked your butt off to earn the money that bought the food that I've been eating for the last 20 years." He replied, "You got that right!"

Yep, I got it right. My dad's decades of labor fed the hungry: me. And it was a work of mercy that he'll be rewarded for in heaven, a work of mercy every breadwinner and home-maker will be rewarded for, provided they do it out of love.

The day I went to work with my dad.

That photo of my dad and me reminds me of another father who is dear to my heart: Fr. Leszek Czelusniak, MIC. "Father Lesh," as we call him here in the United States, is a breadwinner and homemaker in a very literal sense. As a Marian missionary to Rwanda, Africa, he continues to serve in the aftermath of the horrific 1994 genocide that saw the systematic massacre of nearly a million Rwandans in just 100 days (20 percent of the country's population). Since the killings, he and his fellow Marian missionaries have lived a rather intense life of mercy, caring for orphans, rebuilding homes and schools, encouraging forgiveness, feeding the hungry, and giving drink to the thirsty.

Regarding feeding the hungry, Fr. Lesh once remarked to a visitor on a humanitarian trip from the U.S., Ron Schoenfeld, that the children he serves love bread, but "they only get it about once a year." Shocked by this statement, Ron decided to do something. With the support of his local community in Wisconsin, including a $100,000 donation from the Green Bay Packers football team, he didn't settle on buying bread for the town of Kibeho, Rwanda. Rather, he and the Marian

Fathers built a bakery and trained the people on how to use it. Now, the children in the town and beyond don't just have bread once a year but *every day*. It's no surprise to see their happy faces — it may also be no surprise that the same season the Packers made their donation, they won the Super Bowl.

Fr. Lesh with the children he serves in Kibeho, Rwanda.

Father Lesh didn't stop with the bread. Knowing that Kibeho, like many towns in developing parts of the world, does not have a safe and adequate water supply, he traveled to the Midwest to ask several Marian-run parishes for more help. After seeing the photos of the schoolchildren of Kibeho, who had to walk several miles just to get a pitcher of water, the kids at All Saints Catholic School in Kenosha, Wisconsin, responded. They held a Walking for Water fundraiser in the parking lot of their school and raised enough money for Fr. Lesh to purchase two 2,642-gallon water tanks to catch rainwater, which help the schoolchildren he serves.

The point in telling these stories is twofold: (1) There is a real need in developing countries for an adequate supply of nourishing food and safe, accessible drinking water; (2)

there are creative ways through which every one of us can get involved and help, from burly Super Bowl champs to little kids in grade school.

CONTINUE THE STORY...

> *For a video on the day I went to work with my dad, videos and articles on Fr. Lesh and his work in Rwanda, an article on the Walk for Water, and more, visit* **MercyPages.org** *and click "Continue the Story."*

~ Action Items ~
'I Was Hungry and You Gave Me Food;
I Was Thirsty and You Gave Me Drink'

[Check the box next to any of the action items below
that you might actually be able to do.]

☐ My work as a breadwinner or homemaker feeds others besides myself, and I will more consciously do such work as an act of mercy. In other words, I will add the secret ingredient of love.

☐ I will check to see whether or not there is a soup kitchen or food pantry in my area, and I will look into donating food or becoming a volunteer.

  → How will you check? _____

  → When will you check? _____

  → When might you volunteer? _____

☐ I will look into starting a food pantry at my parish.

  → Who will you speak with? _____

  → Who might help you? _____

☐ If one of my neighbors or fellow parishioners becomes debilitated due to grief, an illness, injury, pregnancy, or family crisis, I will offer to make him or her a meal.

  ☐ If the debilitating situation is prolonged, I will look into organizing a group of people to make the meals on a weekly or bi-weekly rotation.

☐ I will check with my parish priest or diocese to find out if there are any poor families or shut-ins in my area who would appreciate my doing some shopping for them.

☐ I will give drink to the thirsty by supporting the efforts of _____ to bring safe and accessible drinking water to developing countries. I will look into the possibility of organizing a "Walk

for Water" at my parish or school to help fund a clean water project in _____
[Visit MercyPages.org under "I Was Hungry… I Was Thirsty."]

☐ I will pray that the seriously ill or handicapped who cannot feed and hydrate themselves will stop being deprived of food and drink. [The tragic case of Terri Schiavo in 2005 is but one example of this ongoing tragedy. It is never right to deprive the sick or the handicapped of food and drink.]

☐ If I ever hear of a situation where someone who is seriously ill or handicapped is being deprived of food or drink, I will inform their caregivers that nourishment and hydration do not constitute extraordinary means of patient care, despite what some healthcare facilities or healthcare professionals might say. Nourishment and hydration are always part of the ordinary care of the sick and handicapped, and receiving such care is a basic right according to God's law. [Visit MercyPages.org under "I Was Hungry… I Was Thirsty."]

CHAPTER TWO

'I Was a Stranger and You Welcomed Me'

This second Scriptural category covers two corporal and two spiritual works of mercy. We'll start first with the corporal works of mercy: "shelter the homeless" and "bury the dead." Then, we'll look at the spiritual works of mercy: "bear wrongs patiently" and "forgive offenses willingly." Actually, before all this, let's look at the plain and obvious point before it escapes us: "*welcome the stranger.*"

W ELCOME THE STRANGER. It seems to me that people today are often so cold, distant, and unfriendly in public places. When I go to the store, for instance, people rarely smile. It's like they're all in their own little worlds, oblivious to everyone else. Scratch that. It's like *we* are all in our own little worlds. I'm guilty of it, too. In fact, I often catch myself and then think: "What the heck… I'm a priest! Smile at people! Greet them! Jesus loves them!" And if you're not a priest, you can still say something similar: "What the heck… I'm a Christian! Smile at people! Greet them! Jesus loves them!"

We should radiate Christ's love, especially when we see people who seem particularly wrapped up in the darkness of our self-absorbed culture. We should welcome them with the warmth of Christ, even if it's as simple as a smile. Yeah, we should practice "the apostolate of smiling." Let me tell a quick story about this.

A close friend of mine loves the beauty and solemnity of the Extraordinary Form of the Mass in Latin, so much so that every Sunday he used to drive to one of the few parishes that offer it. While he absolutely loved the liturgy itself, he was deeply dismayed that the people at the parish often seemed so cold. After Mass, for instance, many of them looked somber, serious, and even unhappy.

Well, one day after Mass, he came up with an idea. With the permission of the pastor, he made photocopies of a leaflet from the 1920s called "The Apostolate of Smiling" by Fr. Bruno Hagspiel, SVD, which encourages people to be friendly and warm toward one another. Then, he passed out the leaflets before Mass. (Unfortunately, it didn't make much of a difference.) Later, he told me the story and showed me a copy of the leaflet. As I began to read it, I couldn't help laughing as I imagined it going into the hands of those sour-faced Christians. But as I continued reading, the laugh was on me. I thought, "Shoot. I don't really practice this, either."

Check it out. Yes, it's a bit corny, but there's something deeply beautiful about it, too. It's a perfect reminder for those of us who are tempted not to welcome the stranger:

The Apostolate of Smiling

Just a little smile on your lips:
>   Cheers your heart
>   Keeps you in good humor
>   Preserves peace in your soul
>   Promotes your health
>   Beautifies your face
>   Induces kindly thoughts
>   Inspires kindly deeds.

SMILE TO YOURSELF...
>   Until you notice that your constant
>   seriousness or even severity has vanished.

SMILE TO YOURSELF...
>   Until you have warmed your own heart with
>   the sunshine of your cheery countenance.
>   Then... go out — and radiate your smile.

THAT SMILE...   ☺
>   Has work to do — work to do for God.

You are an apostle now, and your smile is your instrument for winning souls.

Sanctifying grace dwelling in your soul will give the special charm to your smile that will render it productive of much good.

SMILE — on the lonely faces
SMILE — on the timid faces
SMILE — on the sorrowful faces
SMILE — on the sickly faces
SMILE — on the fresh, young faces
SMILE — on the wrinkled, old faces
SMILE — on the familiar faces of your family and
          friends — let all enjoy the beauty and
          inspiring cheer of your smiling face.

COUNT...
if you will, the number of smiles your smile has drawn from others in one day. The number will represent how many times you have promoted contentment, joy, satisfaction, encouragement, or confidence in the hearts of others. These good dispositions always give birth to unselfish acts and noble deeds. The influence of your smile is spreading, though you do not always see the wonders it is working.

YOUR SMILE...
can bring new life and hope and courage into the hearts of the weary, the overburdened, the discouraged, the tempted, the despairing.

YOUR SMILE...
can help to develop vocations if you are a priest, a brother, or a sister.

YOUR SMILE...
can be the beginning of conversions to the faith.

YOUR SMILE...
can prepare the way for a sinner's return to God.

YOUR SMILE...
Can win for you a host of devoted friends.

SMILE, TOO, AT GOD...
Smile at God in loving acceptance of whatever he
sends into your life, and you will merit to have the
radiantly Smiling Face of Christ gaze on you with
special love throughout eternity.

That's surely a message worth remembering. But maybe
you already practice this. Maybe you're one of those blessed
people who *already* has a natural gift for making the stranger
feel welcome. In other words, maybe you're typically known
for your warm and outgoing personality as well as compassion
and empathy for others. If that describes you, you may want to
pursue the ministry of hospitality as a work of mercy, perhaps
as a greeter in the vestibule of the church before Mass, as part
of the RCIA team at your parish, or through a similar role as a
volunteer in some religious, civic, or service organization such
as the Knights of Columbus that does outreach in your diocese
or area.

Now, before moving on to the next section, I'd like to
share about a work of mercy that's very dear to my heart, one
that has to do with welcoming the stranger — who is the priest.

When I was in the seminary, I remember seeing lots of
books and pamphlets that trumpeted the glories of the priesthood. Designed to promote priestly vocations, they presented
an exalted idea of the priesthood, describing the priest as one
who brings heaven down to earth, as one who blesses, heals,
and sanctifies souls, as one whose humanity gets taken up by
God as an instrument of salvation for the human race.

Now, all of that is true. However, something was missing, something that also gets to the core of the priesthood,
something that I felt in my heart as soon as I discerned my
own call. I couldn't exactly put my finger on it, though, until
I read the following insightful words from a spiritual mother

for priests, Catherine Dougherty, whose cause for sainthood is under way:

> To be a priest is to be indeed called by God, for as he says clearly, "I have chosen you; you have not chosen me." It is also to be the Son of God, for he said, "Thou art my son" and "thou art a priest forever in the line of Melchizedek." Do you know what that means? *It means you will be all his, but that your life will be the loneliest on this earth, naturally speaking; that you will walk shrouded in loneliness, amidst multitudes … .* Do you understand now, in the flower of your youth, what you are asked to do, to be? Slowly, your life will pattern itself on his.[7]

As I read these words, I thought to myself, "She gets it. She understands." Indeed, she understood that while every person on the face of the earth must carry the cross of a "restless heart" because we're made for God, the priest is especially called to carry this cross. Why? Because the priest is called to be another Christ, to take on the Heart of Jesus in a unique and most profound way. And what is in the Heart of Jesus? As Blessed Mother Teresa taught, the heart of the Heart of Jesus is his burning thirst for souls, his terrible thirst, his ardent longing for the love of each and every one of us. And as Mother Teresa further reported, this thirst can be excruciatingly painful … and beautiful. Painful, because it's a deep ache of loneliness and longing. Beautiful, because it's a gateway to profound intimacy with Christ. As one friend paradoxically put it, to not run away from the thirst, to not flee to distractions and creature comforts, is to experience the bittersweet beauty of being "together alone" with the Savior. And that is the wonderful and potentially terrifying invitation that Jesus offers to all his priests.

I think that today, when so many priests no longer have the blessing of being able to share the duties of a parish with other priests and often have to cover two, three, or even four parishes, there's a danger that the invitation to solitude with Christ will feel crushing. While I myself am blessed to live in a loving community of fellow priests and brothers, my heart goes out to the many priests who live alone. So, here, I'm recommending that people be mindful of their priests, support them with prayer, and especially avoid tearing them down with malicious gossip. Of course, many of us priests are very far from perfect, but Satan is always on the lookout for ways to destroy priests with discouragement, and he would love to borrow our tongues to do so.

In closing this section, I'd like to share something that happened just recently.

A woman came to the National Shrine of The Divine Mercy, and we got to talking. With evident love, she shared that she had dedicated her life to praying and sacrificing for priests. She related that she visits priests in retirement homes who are dying and who have no one to visit them and that she supports priests with words of encouragement. Finally, she said to me with grave seriousness, "Father, can I entrust to you a very special intention?"

I said, "Sure."

She continued, "Well, we're here at the National Shrine of The Divine Mercy, and there's a particular group of priests from my diocese who are in great need of mercy. Would you pray for them?"

"Yes," I replied.

So, she brought out a list of seven names and said, "These are the priests of my diocese who have committed suicide."

I looked at the list, and my heart broke. I could tell from the love and concern in her eyes that hers was broken, too. Then, I thought to myself, "If the Church had more spiritual mothers like this, nearly every priest would become a saint." Yes, what a beautiful vocation it is to be a spiritual mother to priests, to be one of those women who welcome the priests as their very dear sons, the priests who often feel like strangers in this world.

SHELTER THE HOMELESS. This is a tough one. I mean, it's probably not prudent to open your house to just any homeless person on the street, especially if you have a family. Also, most of us don't have the means to provide homes for the homeless. So do we just skip this point? No. First of all, there are a lot of things we can do for the homeless, materially speaking, which we'll consider later under the "Action Items" below. Second, and this is very important, we can shelter the homeless by welcoming them, "the stranger," into the home of our hearts. To help explain this, I'd like to tell a story about my friend, Eric Mahl.

In college, Eric was known as "Eric the Mauler" or "Ani-Mahl" because of his tenacity on the football field. In the NFL, he was known as the toughest, hardest worker on the team. As a converted Christian, he's one of the most remarkable people I know.

Following his conversion, Eric left professional football, lived in the world for a brief time, and then entered a monastery where he lived as a hermit. After three years of silence, penance, and prayer, he experienced a call from the Lord to "bring Divine Mercy to the poor." Then, he heard the words, "Now, go to the National Shrine of The Divine Mercy and present yourself to Fr. Joseph."

Eric had never been to the National Shrine before and didn't know who Fr. Joseph was, but he obeyed because the call was so strong and clear.

With the blessing of his superior, he left the hermitage, went home to his family in Ohio, and then, he and his dad came out to the Shrine.

After arriving at the Shrine, Eric began his search for Fr. Joseph. To his surprise (and, probably, great disappointment!), he soon discovered that "Fr. Joseph" is the honorary title given to the director of the Association of Marian Helpers, who is me. So, Eric came to my office and explained his desire to bring Divine Mercy to the poor. Because the Marians at the Shrine didn't have a direct outreach to the poor at the time, I recommended various communities that did and gave Eric my blessing.

Eric visited those communities but didn't feel they were a good fit. So, he went back to Ohio and, to be faithful to his call, chose to live on the streets of Cleveland with the homeless.

At first, many of the homeless thought he was an undercover cop. They'd ask him, "Why are you here?"

He'd say, "Because God wants me to be your brother."

"Oh, so you want to help the homeless."

"No," Eric would say, "I want to love them."

And that's what Eric did. He listened to their problems, prayed with them, and shared their life of hunger, loneliness, and cold — especially the cold, and I'm not just talking about the weather.

Eric tells me that when he played for the Cleveland Browns, he'd go to Mass sometimes in the city, and afterward, people would be so friendly and eager to meet him. But later, when he was living with the homeless and his clothes were worn and dirty, face unshaven, and hair disheveled, some of the same previously friendly people didn't recognize him and would completely ignore him, even when he smiled and tried to talk with them. He said that that was the hardest part of living on the streets: peoples' coldness. They would say unkind things to him, express their disapproval when he'd enter the church to pray, and sometimes act as if he weren't even human. Sadly, all of these people were Christians.

After a year on the streets, Eric felt a call to return to the National Shrine of The Divine Mercy and to present himself to Fr. Joseph again. On the very day he arrived, I had just asked the Lord to send us someone for our ministry. So it was really amazing, and long story short, Eric joined the Marian Fathers as a lay member and now runs our outreach to those in need.

Anyway, when I told him I was writing this book, Eric said to make sure I tell everyone to please treat the homeless as human beings. He explained that most of them just want someone to look them in the eye, say hello, or listen to their stories. Finally, he concluded with the following:

You don't have to give them money, and often that's not a good idea, but at least give them a little bit of your time and recognize their dignity in the way you look at them and talk to them. So many people ignore the homeless, yet when you treat them with respect and love, it restores their dignity, and that's true mercy.

In short, Eric reminds us to shelter the homeless not necessarily with our homes but with our hearts — and with a grin, he'd add, "Don't forget the apostolate of smiling!"

Eric Mahl on the streets of Cleveland shortly before joining the Marians.

*B*URY THE DEAD. This is another tough one. I mean, I don't see this as a big problem today. What family doesn't bury their deceased loved ones? And surely the authorities aren't just going to let a dead body remain unburied. So do we simply skip this point? No. There are other ways that we can bury the dead. (By the end of this section, it will be clear why this topic falls under the category "Welcome the Stranger.")

First, we can attend funerals. Since I started my position as "Fr. Joseph," I've attended a lot of funerals for the relatives of the people who work in our office. Of course, I go to all their funerals, unless I'm out of town — it's my job... I'm a priest! But I've also noticed that there are always a group of people from our office who attend nearly every single wake and funeral. In many cases, they hardly know the person who died or are only loosely acquainted with the relatives. Well, their generosity in being present is a beautiful witness and comfort to the family. In fact, I often hear the family say such things as, "I was so touched by how many people from the office came." This is a work of mercy that pleases the Lord. And even if the family doesn't notice you at the funeral, the deceased person sees you, and God sees you. It truly is a way of "welcoming the stranger."

Another way of welcoming the stranger that's related to funerals is to be sensitive to those who are grieving. After the funeral is over and everyone has gone home, people often take a long time to emotionally "bury the dead," and they usually appreciate when others acknowledge their pain. I've heard many grieving people complain that because their friends and relatives don't know what to say, they often don't say anything at all. They just disappear for a while. Then, those who are grieving feel like strangers in their pain, strangers without any welcome. But it doesn't take much to welcome them. Simply letting them know that you are thinking of them and praying for them means a lot.

In my community, the Marian Fathers of the Immaculate Conception, we have a long tradition of praying for the deceased, and we offer spiritual enrollments for people who have died. Essentially, these are sympathy cards that include a promise of prayer and a sharing in the spiritual benefits of the Marian Fathers. Little gestures such as giving a sympathy card can mean so much to those who are grieving, and it's a way of burying the dead and welcoming a stranger.

A sympathy enrollment card, with its promise of prayer,
can mean so much to a grieving loved one.

Another way we can "bury the dead" is to be prayerfully present at an abortion clinic. Let me illustrate this with a story.

When I was in college, I literally walked across the country (coast to coast) with a group of friends to raise money for women in crisis pregnancies and to be a prayerful presence at the abortion clinics along the way. After several weeks of walking and praying at different clinics, though, I began to feel so helpless. Despite the efforts of the sidewalk counselors in our group to try and convince the mothers to keep their babies or put them up for adoption, there were rarely any "saves." And so, I was tempted to think it was a waste of time to be there at the clinics. After all, I felt I couldn't do anything for the babies (or for the mothers and fathers who would be so wounded by the abortions).

But one day, as I stood in front of a clinic, silently praying the Rosary, I imagined myself on Calvary with Mary as her Son was dying. I thought to myself, "It is good to be here. Even if nobody sees this or cares, it's the right thing to do, and God sees it, and he cares." I also realized that the dignity of the unborn children calls for someone to be there as a witness. Of course, I didn't know the babies, but just being there was a way of welcoming the stranger into heaven with a prayerful, loving presence.

Related to this point about abortion and burying the dead is the beautiful work of mercy of reaching out to the living victims of abortion, such as the baby's mother and father. So many of these mothers and fathers experience excruciating spiritual and emotional agony after abortion. And while they surely don't bury their babies, they do bury their pain — but it doesn't stay buried. It rises up in the form of self-loathing, suicidal tendencies, and other self-destructive behavior. After abortion, these mothers and fathers often become unwelcome strangers to themselves, and it can be a powerful work of mercy to introduce them to post-abortion healing resources, such as Project Rachel and Rachel's Vineyard.

*B*EAR *WRONGS PATIENTLY.* "Wrongs" can be little things like interruptions of our work or dealing with long-winded friends. The problem comes when these little things start to get to us. Then, impatience can well up in our hearts, and if we're not careful, it can make even our closest loved ones or co-workers feel like unwelcome strangers. If we let it in, impatience changes our body language, our face, and our words into the opposite of welcoming. In the long run, such impatience may not seem like much of a big deal, but it is. Why? Because the same people who annoy us are Christ, and our attitude toward them is our attitude toward the Lord, who will one day say, "You did it to me. ... You were welcoming to me even when you were tempted to make me a stranger." Or he will say, "You did *not* do it to me. ... You were impatient with me when nobody else would welcome me, and you sent me away." May we never hear that! May we strive for patience with the people who cause us to bear the "little wrongs."

The following two examples from the life of St. Faustina, which show her own efforts to bear the little wrongs, can help us as we also strive to be patient with others:

There is a woman here who was once one of our students. Naturally, she puts my patience to the test. She comes to see me several times a day. After each of these visits I am tired out, but I see that the Lord Jesus has sent that soul to me. Let everything glorify You, O Lord. Patience gives glory to God.[8]

During meditation, the sister on the kneeler next to mine keeps coughing and clearing her throat, sometimes without a break. It occurred to me once that I might take another place for the time of the meditation, because Mass had already been offered. But then I thought that if I did change my place, the sister would notice this and might feel hurt that I had moved away from her. So I decided to continue in prayer in my usual place, and to offer this act of patience to God. Toward the end of the meditation, my soul was flooded with God's consolation, and this to the limit of what my heart could bear; and the Lord gave me to know that if I had moved away from that sister I would have moved away also from those graces that flowed into my soul.[9]

Now, as for the big wrongs, I think the best way to treat them is with a personal example.

Recently, I experienced a difficult situation where someone became very upset and decided to take it out on me verbally. The person said offensive things, lied repeatedly, and tried to provoke me to anger. By the grace of God, I remained calm, listened, and then responded with firmness but also love, which defused the situation and helped bring it to a happy conclusion.

Afterward, I could hardly believe it, because I have a bit of an irascible temperament, and it's difficult for me not to push back in the face of injustice. Others who observed this verbal attack and know me well were also surprised that I remained so calm.

It's not always easy to remain calm.

From that situation, I realized more deeply there's a real power of grace that comes from remaining at peace and not stooping to the level of those who attack us. Of course, prudence may dictate that we defend ourselves, and sometimes we have a moral obligation to do so. But there's much to be said for controlling our emotions and responding to injustice with patience and mercy. Of course, this is not easy, but if we ask God's help, reflect on how Christ responded to those who attacked him, and strive to be patient in the small things, we ourselves will grow in patience and have a better chance of not blowing up in the face of blatant wrongs.

To conclude this point, let's reflect on the following dialogue between Jesus and St. Faustina about bearing wrongs patiently:

> **My pupil, have great love for those who cause you suffering. Do good to those who hate you.** I answered, "O my Master, you see very well that I feel no love for them, and that troubles me." Jesus answered, **It is not always within your power to**

control your feelings. **You will recognize that you have love if, after having experienced annoyance and contradiction, you do not lose your peace, but pray for those who have made you suffer and wish them well.**[10]

*F*ORGIVE OFFENSES WILLINGLY. To forgive is to welcome back those who, through their wrongs toward us, have become like strangers to us in our hearts. This is so important! If we refuse to forgive, we will be like strangers to the Lord, and he will not welcome us. This may sound harsh, but it's a painful truth of the Gospel, "For the measure you give will be the measure you get back" (Lk 6:38). Also, we pray in the Our Father, "Forgive us our trespasses *as we forgive those who trespass against us.*"

To help us root out the lack of forgiveness in our lives, which blocks us from heaven, let's make a special examination of conscience on this topic now, realizing that we need not get discouraged or despair if we struggle in this area. For, if we have even the slightest bit of good will, the Lord's mercy is there for us. Moreover, we should keep in mind that it often takes time for us to be able to forgive fully, and the Lord is patient. O Lord, please give us the grace to forgive!

Are there people in my life whom I haven't forgiven? Do I hold on to bitterness over past wounds? Am I resentful toward anyone? Is there anyone to whom I give the silent treatment? Is there anyone I would refuse to help if he needed it? Do I pray for my enemies? Is there anyone for whom I would not pray? Do I need to ask anyone for forgiveness? Is there anyone with whom it might be helpful to talk regarding a past hurt that especially bothers me, and can I do so without being accusatory and with a readiness to forgive? Have I asked Jesus for the grace to forgive?

Do I reflect on how often Jesus has forgiven me? Do I reflect on his example of forgiving those who crucified him? Do I realize my sins crucified him? Do I realize he still loves me when I choose to forgive but struggle with forgetting? Do

I try to forget? Or do I continually replay in my mind past hurts? Do I try to give people a clean slate? Have I said, "I forgive you"? Do I try to forgive? Or do I give in to anger, which seeks to do evil to someone out of a desire for revenge? According to St. Faustina, "We resemble God most when we forgive our neighbors."[11]

Pope John Paul II forgives the man who shot him.

CONTINUE THE STORY...

To learn more about walking across the country for life, Eric Mahl's story, and more, visit **MercyPages.org** *and click "Continue the Story."*

~ Action Items ~
'I Was a Stranger and You Welcomed Me'

Welcome the Stranger...

☐ I will practice the Apostolate of Smiling. I will do so at the following places:

 ☐ At home

 ☐ At church

 ☐ At work

 ☐ In public

 ☐ Other: _____

☐ I enjoy welcoming the stranger and newcomers. I will consider participating in...

 ☐ A ministry of hospitality in my parish, such as a greeter.

 ☐ The RCIA team at my parish.

 ☐ Volunteer opportunities in hospitality and community outreach in my area or diocese by contacting local civic, service, and cultural organizations whose mission would be a good fit for me.

☐ I will support priests. I will do so...

 ☐ By resolving never to tear down a priest with gossip.

 ☐ By praying for them.

  → What prayer?_____

  → When? _____

 ☐ By sacrificing for them.

  → What sacrifice? _____

 ☐ By supporting them with good deeds such as offering to make a meal for them, inviting them to dinner with my family, or writing them a word of encouragement.

→ I will support them with the good deed of...

_____

☐ By looking into becoming a "spiritual mother" for priests. [You can find more information about spiritual motherhood for priests by visiting MercyPages.org under "Welcome the Stranger." Also, I share more about this beautiful vocation in my book, *The 'One Thing' Is Three*, pages 280-283.]

☐ Other: _____

☐ If someone moves into my neighborhood, I will make an effort to visit and offer a housewarming gift, such as homemade cookies or bread.

☐ Remembering that Jesus, Mary, and Joseph were once immigrants and that my own ancestors were likely immigrants as well, I will strive to be particularly friendly, warm, and welcoming to this kind of "stranger."

☐ I will examine my conscience to see if I have let any prejudice, bigotry, or racism poison my heart. If I have, I will tell the Lord I'm sorry and resolve to welcome the stranger.

Shelter the Homeless...

☐ I will investigate whether or not there is a homeless shelter in my area. If there is, I will call or pay a visit to see how I might help.

☐ I will help the homeless people I may run into on the street. I will do so by...

　☐ Purchasing a package of nutritious bars or a similar type of food, reserving it for the homeless, and taking a bar or two with me when I know I may run into someone who is homeless.

　☐ Stopping to listen to a homeless person and striving to radiate the love of Christ and see Christ in him or her, provided it's not an unsafe environment.

☐ Investigating whether Habitat for Humanity (or a similar organization) is active in my area. [Habitat for Humanity is a non-profit organization that coordinates and helps fund the building of affordable housing for the homeless in local communities.] If it is, I will see if I can donate my time or help in some other way in building affordable houses for the homeless in my community. [Visit MercyPages.org under "Shelter the Homeless."]

Bury the Dead…

☐ I will consider going to the funeral of…

  ☐ Those with whom I am only loosely associated.

  ☐ A total stranger.

☐ I will call or write to a friend who is grieving.
[Recommendation: Give them the gift of prayer by sending an enrollment sympathy card. For more information, see the Resource Pages at the end of this book.]

☐ I will pray outside an abortion clinic.

  ☐ I will check with my diocese or local pro-life organization to find out when others will gather to pray at any clinics in my area.

  ☐ I will consider getting trained to be a sidewalk counselor. [Visit MercyPages.org under "Bury the Dead."]

  ☐ I will sign up to coordinate a 40 Days for Life vigil site. [Visit MercyPages.org under "Bury the Dead."]

☐ I will learn about post-abortion healing resources such as Project Rachel and Rachel's Vineyard.
[Visit MercyPages.org under "Bury the Dead."]

  ☐ I will recommend a Rachel's Vineyard healing retreat to someone I know who has had an abortion.

  ☐ I will look into volunteering at a Rachel's Vineyard retreat.

Bear Wrongs Patiently...

☐ The next time I feel impatience welling up in my heart, I will think of Jesus' words, "You did it to me," and I will strive to be patient with Christ in the members of his Body.

☐ The next time I am unjustly attacked, I will strive to remain calm with the peace of Christ and respond with love.

Forgive Offenses Willingly...

☐ I will forgive those who have hurt me.

    → Who do I need to forgive? [Don't write it down. Just think about it.]

    ☐ I will confess my lack of forgiveness.

        → When? _____

        → Where? _____

    ☐ I will pray the Chaplet of Divine Mercy for the person or people I need to forgive (or some other prayer). [See Appendix Two to learn how to pray the chaplet.]

    ☐ I will make an effort to stop replaying in my mind the hurt that others have put me through. I will strive to let it go and pray for them instead.

    ☐ I'm having a hard time forgiving. Therefore, I will learn more about how to forgive. [Visit MercyPages.org under "Forgive Offenses Willingly."]

CHAPTER THREE

'I Was Naked and You Clothed Me'

This third Scriptural category covers one corporal and three spiritual works of mercy. The corporal work of mercy is "clothe the naked." The spiritual works are "instruct the ignorant," "counsel the doubtful," and "comfort the afflicted." Let's start with the corporal work of mercy.

CLOTHE THE NAKED. Regarding clothing the naked, I think the problem in Western countries today is not so much that people don't have enough clothes to wear but that they have too many. Chances are all of us have more clothes in our closets than we need. Well, a good work of mercy is to donate some of our clothes to one of the many groups that distribute them to the needy. This is common-sense mercy, and it's easy to do since we all probably get invited to participate in a clothing drive at least annually. So, I suggest that the bigger issue under this category are the *spiritual* works of mercy that involve "clothing the naked," which we turn to now.

Most of our closets probably look like this.

INSTRUCT THE IGNORANT. Let me begin by making a clarification. While in Western countries there are usually more than enough clothes to go around, at the same time, these days, there seems to be a big problem with *nakedness.* In other words, at least where I'm from in sunny Southern California, people often forget to put on their clothes, even at Mass! Of course, they're not totally naked, but they don't leave much to the imagination.

At my home parish in LA, it's gotten so bad that the pastor has had to put up a big sign with diagrams at the entrance to the church, reminding people that shorts, bare bellies, and skin-tight clothing are inappropriate for Mass. So, what we're dealing with here is not poverty (lack of clothing) but ignorance (lack of knowledge about clothing). And one of the ways we can "clothe the naked" is to tactfully teach our children and our friends about modesty in dress, letting them know that despite what "everybody else is doing," some things are still meant to be covered or hidden.[12]

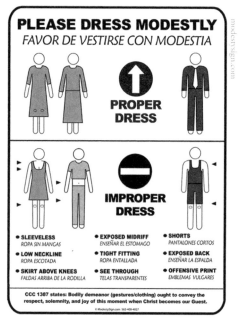

The modesty sign at my home parish in LA.

Actually, "clothing the naked" by giving instruction is a work of mercy that applies not only to teaching others about modesty but about all the virtues. In fact, when he instructs us on the virtues, St. Paul says to "clothe yourselves" with virtues such as "compassion, kindness, lowliness, meekness, and patience ... and above all, clothe yourselves with love" (Col 3:12-14). So, teaching people about what is right and wrong, clothing their ignorance through instruction, is a form of mercy — and for parents, it's a solemn obligation. In light of this, we can ask ourselves whether or not we clothe the naked in our families and communities by having the courage to share the truth with them. For, indeed, without the truth, we cannot live the virtues that spiritually clothe and adorn us with holiness.

But, you may say, "I'm not good at explaining things" or "I'm afraid I'll get it all wrong and turn people off to the truth." Alright, no problem. One thing we can do, as we grow in the faith ourselves, is to let others speak for us. Let me explain.

When I was in high school, I was pretty naked. I mean, I hardly knew anything about my Catholic faith and how to live it. At one point during that time, my mom and my sister experienced a renewal in their faith and would constantly lecture me about the teachings of the Church. I didn't want to hear it and wrote the two of them off as religious fanatics. Well, after a while, they wised up and changed their tactics. They pretty much left me alone, but they would strategically drop booklets and pamphlets around the house for me to pick up and read and tapes for me to listen to. (This was before CDs.)

Their plan worked. I picked up one of the tapes and listened to it in the privacy of my car. Of all topics, it had to do with the Catholic Church's teaching on artificial contraception. When I first found the tape, I was actually thinking something like, "Well, this should be good for a laugh. Now I'll get to hear just how crazy and out of touch our Church really is." But it wasn't crazy. To my surprise, it made a lot of sense, and the way it explained the beauty of marriage and human sexuality totally blew me away. It had a deep effect on me and helped kick off my conversion.

That all happened about 20 years ago, and since that time, the resources available to Catholics are off-the-charts amazing. There are so many great books, CDs, study programs, and retreats. We're really spoiled now. We can clothe the whole world!

Among the different organizations that offer such resources, one stands out for me in terms of the high quality of their products and inexpensive prices: Lighthouse Catholic Media. Lighthouse is a non-profit organization that specializes in producing audio CDs and MP3s to educate Catholics in their faith. The CDs are only about $4 each and the MP3 downloads are even less than that. Also, they have hundreds of talks from some of the best Catholic speakers today. I highly recommend checking out their website (LighthouseCatholicMedia.org), ordering a CD, joining their CD of the Month Club, or downloading an MP3. Also, if you're not computer savvy or can't wait to get the CD in the mail, just check out your parish or one near you that has a Lighthouse Catholic Media kiosk. (Such kiosks are in the back of nearly half of the parishes in the U.S.) And if your parish doesn't already have a kiosk, you might ask your pastor about getting one to help clothe the parish's nakedness. (Well, I wouldn't quite put it to him that way.)

Look for a kiosk like this at a parish near you.

COUNSEL THE DOUBTFUL; COMFORT THE AFFLICTED. Doubt, discouragement, and despair — the three "d's"— are among the worst afflictions. One leads right into the next, and this downward spiral brings us to hell, both figuratively and literally. Like ignorance, these are forms of spiritual nakedness, and like ignorance, they need to be clothed. A most powerful work of mercy is to nip these three d's in the bud by stopping doubt before it sprouts into discouragement and then blossoms into the black orchid of despair, destroyer of the spiritual life. A most powerful work of mercy is to combat doubt by deepening faith, also known as trust.

What is it that people doubt? Of course, they doubt whether God is real, whether there is a heaven or a hell, and whether Christianity is true. But I think the worst kind of doubt-affliction has to do with God's love and mercy. To put it bluntly: That's where Satan focuses his attacks. It seems it's easier for him to get someone to doubt God's love than it is to get the same person to doubt God's existence, and the result may even be better for him! I mean, a person may not believe in God but still feel loved, and that love can open up to a living faith. But if a person believes in God yet thinks God doesn't love him, has rejected him, and can't wait to punish him, then that may be a worse situation. When Satan brings someone to that place, then he can easily lead the person down the dark path of discouragement and despair. So, again, his target is getting people to doubt God's love and mercy.

In our day, in our society, I believe people doubt God's love and mercy more than ever before, and I think it's related to the unprecedented proliferation of sin. It's not that people don't believe in God. I think that, for the most part, they still do. It's just that they give in to many of the temptations to sin in our day and then think God has rejected them and no longer loves them. They believe their sins are too dark for the light of God's mercy to forgive them. So, they continue on the path of sin and turn away from God.

Well, because of this sad situation, God has given us a special gift for our time. It's called the Divine Mercy message and devotion, which I mentioned earlier. It comes to us through St. Faustina Kowalska, and far from being some new kind of Gospel, it's rather a reminder of the heart of the Gospel, namely, the mercy of God. It's a reminder that Jesus came not for the self-righteous but for sinners, that our Savior has the heart of the Good Shepherd who will even leave behind the 99 to go out in search of the lost sheep. It's a reminder that, as Jesus told St. Faustina, **"The greater the sinner, the greater the right he has to My mercy."**[13]

Anyway, the message of Divine Mercy has the power to break the grip of doubt that destroys so many souls in our day. And when people hear it, when they hear the good news of God's mercy, it melts their hearts. When they learn that God loves them not because they're so good, polite, talented, church-going and kind but because they need his love — it changes their lives. They realize, "He loves me. He really loves me." They further realize, "He loves me even more because I'm so broken."

The truth of God's mercy is amazingly powerful. I know it. I've seen it. But the big question is how do we communicate it? How do we help clothe people's nakedness? How do we heal the serious affliction that causes us to doubt God's mercy? Obviously, we're not all preachers, and the people who need this message most probably don't want to hear a sermon anyway. Okay, so what can we do? I have two recommendations.

First, practice the "merciful outlook." This is where we allow Jesus to borrow our faces so he can go incognito to the people who have turned their backs on him. It's to allow Jesus to love them through the way we look at them. They probably won't immediately recognize Jesus through such a look, but it can have its healing effect as it prepares hearts to eventually recognize the Lord's loving face. (See Appendix One for more information, including on the "merciful question," which is related to the merciful outlook.)

My second recommendation to help clothe the nakedness of our neighbor's doubt in God's mercy involves a garment that's neither expensive nor difficult to give. It's usually made of paper or canvas, and it's called the Image of Divine Mercy.

The Image of Divine Mercy.

They say a picture is worth a thousand words, and this image, given to us by Jesus himself through St. Faustina, conveys a thousand words of mercy. In it, Jesus doesn't wait for us to come to him. Rather, he comes to us. See him stepping toward you, into your darkness. See how his hand is raised in blessing. See how the rays of love and mercy go out to you to heal you. See how he simply wants you to say to him, "Jesus, I trust in you." That's all he wants. That's all he needs. He takes care of the rest when we turn away from sin and put our trust in him. But don't just take my word for it — take his:

> **I desire that these souls** [who strive for holiness] **distinguish themselves by boundless trust in My mercy. I myself will attend the sanctification of such souls. I will provide them with everything they will need to attain sanctity. The graces of my mercy are drawn by means of one vessel only, and that is — trust. The more a soul trusts, the more it will receive. Souls that trust boundlessly are a great comfort to Me, because I pour all the treasures of My graces into them. I rejoice that they ask for much, because it is My desire to give much, very much. On the other hand, I am sad when souls ask for little, when they narrow their hearts.**[14]

Why am I getting into all of this? Because Jesus wants us all to be saints and apostles of his mercy in these terrible times. He wants us to be living images of his mercy so our witness will help others to overcome their doubt, discouragement, and despair.

One rather painless way you can be an apostle of Divine Mercy is to get yourself some images of Divine Mercy and do "hit-and-runs" with them. In other words, I recommend that you get some business-card-sized Divine Mercy Images, keep them in your wallet or purse, and then, when you see someone who seems stuck in the three d's, tell them, "Jesus loves you" and — BAM! — hand them the little card and make your escape. People really appreciate that. You'd be surprised. And we've made the ammo for these hit-and-runs very inexpensive. We offer these little cards for about a penny each and ship them for free. (Evangelization just got easier.)

Also, I suggest that you don't just do hit-and-runs. Why not also clothe the naked of your whole parish? No, I'm not talking about getting one of those dress-code signs that the pastor at my home parish put up (although that might not be a bad idea). Rather, I'm talking about teaching your whole parish about Divine Mercy. What? How can you do that?

Here's how: Introduce your parish to Divine Mercy Sunday. In other words, help prepare it for a solemn Divine Mercy Sunday celebration, if it doesn't already have one. What's that? Well, the Second Sunday of Easter, thanks to St. Pope John Paul II, is now officially known as "Divine Mercy Sunday." And it is, by far, my favorite day of the year. Why? Because of the special grace that Jesus promises to pour out on everyone who goes to confession (at least sometime during Lent), is in the state of grace, and receives Holy Communion on Divine Mercy Sunday with the intention of receiving this special grace.

Alright, so what is this special grace? Well, the theologian assigned in the 1960s by the future Pope John Paul II to investigate it likened it to a "second Baptism."[15] It's not a Baptism, but it so thoroughly cleanses the soul that it's like getting a totally clean slate. In fact, if you were to die right after receiving it, you wouldn't have to go to purgatory!

Now, if the promise of such a grace isn't something that will help people overcome the doubt that God doesn't love them, then I don't know what will. So why not "clothe the naked" of your parish by helping them to overcome the affliction of doubt, discouragement, and despair through a rejuvenating experience of Divine Mercy? Why not help organize a Divine Mercy Sunday celebration at your parish?

CONTINUE THE STORY...

> *To learn more about the Image of Divine Mercy, Divine Mercy Sunday, St. Faustina, and more, visit* **MercyPages.org** *and click "Continue the Story."*

~ Action Items ~
'I Was Naked and You Clothed Me'

[Check the box next to any of the action items below that you might actually be able to do.]

Clothe the Naked…

☐ I will donate the clothes and shoes I don't need.

    ☐ I will go through my closet on the following date:

    _____

    ☐ I will donate to the following organization:

    _____

☐ I will strive to dress modestly.

    ☐ I will do some research on the Internet to learn more about the value of modesty. [Visit MercyPages.org under "Clothe the Naked."]

    ☐ I will teach my children the value of modesty, first by my own example.

    ☐ I will share with my friends the importance of modesty in dress.

☐ I will offer to buy a modesty sign for my parish or recommend it to my pastor. [Visit MercyPages.org under "Clothe the Naked."]

Instruct the Ignorant…

☐ I will strive to learn more about my Catholic faith.

    ☐ I will search for and purchase good Catholic books. [In my opinion, the best way to find good Catholic books is to visit your local Catholic bookstore. There, you can pick up the books, peruse them, and discover what's right for you. Also, when you purchase from a Catholic bookstore, you support a mercy ministry that truly "instructs the ignorant," a ministry that needs our support more than ever in this age of major Internet book retailers.]

☐ I will find out where the closest Catholic bookstores are to my house and visit them.

→ When? _____

☐ I will take time to read good Catholic books.

→ Which ones? _____

→ When? _____

→ Where? _____

→ For how long per day/week? _____

☐ I will search for and purchase good Catholic CDs or MP3s. [Again, I highly recommend Lighthouse Catholic Media as a resource. You can't beat their selection or prices. Visit LighthouseCatholicMedia.org.]

☐ I will take time to listen to these CDs or MP3s while…

☐ Cleaning

☐ Cooking

☐ Exercising

☐ Driving

☐ Other: _____

☐ I will share my faith with others. I will do so…

☐ By giving or lending good Catholic books and pamphlets.

→ Which books or pamphlets? _____

→ To whom? _____

→ When? _____

[Recommendation: For Protestants who are open to the Catholic faith, one of the best books is *Rome Sweet Home: Our Journey to Catholicism* by Scott and Kimberly Hahn. Also, Lighthouse Catholic Media has CDs of their conversion stories for those who would rather listen than read.

For people who want to grow in holiness as quickly and easily as possible, I recommend that they consecrate themselves to Jesus through Mary. An updated and easy-to-use method is the book *33 Days to Morning Glory*.

Finally, for troubled youth who are struggling with their faith, the most effective tool I've come across is the conversion story of Fr. Donald Calloway, MIC. He tells his story in the book *No Turning Back: A Witness to Mercy.* Lighthouse Catholic Media carries an audio version and Marian Press offers a DVD version.]

☐ By giving or lending good Catholic CDs.

→ Which CDs? _____

→ To whom? _____

→ When? _____

[Recommendation: Browse the Lighthouse Catholic Media website (LighthouseCatholicMedia.org) to find the right CDs for your friends and family.]

☐ By bringing a Lighthouse Catholic Media kiosk to my parish if it doesn't already have one. [For more information, visit their website.]

☐ By leading a small-group parish study or retreat.

→ Which study or retreat? _____

→ When? _____

[Recommendation: Of course, I recommend Hearts Afire: Parish-based Programs from the Marian Fathers of the Immaculate Conception (HAPP®). HAPP offers some of the most popular and inexpensive parish programs. Visit AllHeartsAfire.org.]

☐ By inviting others to a small-group parish study or retreat.

→ Which study or retreat? _____

→ Who will you invite? _____

☐ By doing the following... [What else can you think of to share your faith with others?]

_____

_____

_____

Counsel the Doubtful; Comfort the Afflicted...

☐ I will learn more about the message of Divine Mercy.

    ☐ I will do so by...

_____

[Recommendation: The booklets featured in the Resource Pages, *Divine Mercy Explained* and *The Divine Mercy Image Explained*, present brief yet thorough overviews. The *Diary of St. Faustina* gives the whole picture.]

☐ I will trust more in God's mercy. To help me with this...

    ☐ I will get a Divine Mercy image.

       → From where? _____

[DivineMercyArt.com has the highest quality, biggest selection, and lowest prices. Visit the site or see the Resource Pages at the end of this book for more information.]

       → Which image? [I recommend the "Vilnius Image" (see page 67) because it was painted under the direction of St. Faustina and was the favorite of her spiritual director, Blessed Michael Sopocko. To see examples of the various images, such as the Vilnius, Hyla, and Skemp, visit DivineMercyArt.com.]

          ☐ Vilnius

          ☐ Hyla

          ☐ Skemp

          ☐ Other: _____

       → Which format?

          ☐ Print

          ☐ Canvas

          ☐ Framed or unframed?

       → What size? _____

☐ I will help others to trust in God's mercy.

 ☐ I will do "hit-and-runs." In other words, I will get a box of 1,000 business-card-sized Divine Mercy images and pass them out to friends, family, and total strangers. [Recommendation: Go to DivineMercyArt.com, click "Super Specials," and be amazed at the low price for these cards. Also, the prices on the 8"x10" prints are incredibly low.]

 ☐ I will talk to my pastor about inviting the Marian Fathers' Evangelization Team to give talks on Divine Mercy at my parish. [For more information, call 1-866-895-3236 or e-mail parishmissions@marian.org]

 ☐ If my parish doesn't already have a Divine Mercy Sunday celebration, I will try to bring it to the parish by...

  ☐ Visiting CelebrateMercySunday.org to learn more.

  ☐ Talking or writing to my pastor, asking him to allow a solemn Divine Mercy Sunday celebration at the parish.

  ☐ Volunteering to help organize the celebration.

☐ With my pastor's permission, I will purchase a Divine Mercy image for my parish or ask the pastor to purchase one.

 → From where? _____

 → Which image?

  ☐ Vilnius

  ☐ Hyla

  ☐ Skemp

  ☐ Other _____

 → Which format?

  ☐ Print

  ☐ Canvas

  ☐ Framed or unframed?

 → What size? _____

CHAPTER FOUR

'I Was Sick and You Visited Me'

This fourth Scriptural category covers one corporal work of mercy, "comfort the sick."

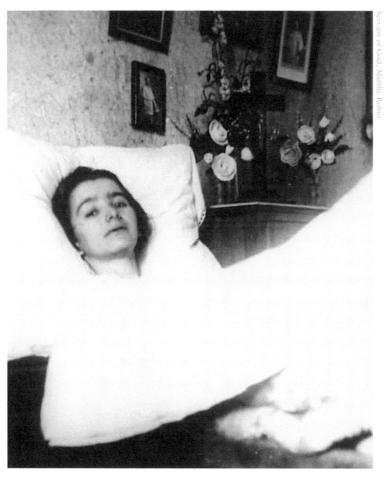

To visit the sick is to visit Christ.

COMFORT THE SICK. "*Comfort the sick? But I don't want to get sick!*" We've all experienced this kind of attitude, either on the giving or receiving end. One family member is sick, and another one won't go within 10 feet of him for fear of being contaminated. Or, if he does come by, he's holding his breath and keeping his distance. And God forbid you cough or sneeze while he's in the room! This is understandable, but somebody has got to help the sick, because the sick person is Christ.

Maybe the problem isn't that we're worried about getting sick. Maybe it's just that it's not always easy to be around those who are suffering — that, at least, has been my experience.

When I used to work at a hospital as a seminarian, I had the hardest time walking into each patient's room. In fact, instead of doing my duty, I was often tempted to just go to the chapel or procrastinate by chatting at the nurses' station. It was hard to face the suffering, to walk into it, to greet it. Because I struggled with this, I felt like such a failure. "How can I become a priest," I thought, "when I can hardly face the sick?"

Later, I was comforted to read that one of my heroes, Karol Wojtyla (later St. Pope John Paul II), also had to confront this challenge:

> I remember that at the beginning the sick intimidated me. I needed a lot of courage to stand before a sick person and enter, so to speak, into his physical and spiritual pain, not to betray discomfort, and to show at least a little loving compassion.

That's exactly how I felt! Whew. When I first read those words, I figured there was hope for me, especially when I read what follows. John Paul goes on to share a discovery that takes him beyond his initial discomfort.

> Only later did I begin to grasp the profound meaning of the mystery of human suffering. In the weakness of the sick, I saw emerging ever more clearly a new strength — *the strength of mercy.* In a sense, the sick provoke mercy. ... By their illness and suffering they call forth acts of mercy and create the possibility for accomplishing them.[16]

Ah, so here's a key to the mystery of why it's often so hard to see suffering. It calls us out of ourselves. It challenges us to forget ourselves, to leave the comfort of our egos, to think of another and suffer with him. Yet, when we accept the invitation to take that step out of ourselves, we get taken up by "the strength of mercy," which brings us, almost effortlessly, to carry out acts of love and compassion.

We've all experienced "the strength of mercy." It captures us, unexpectedly, at different moments of our lives. For instance, we see a look of sorrow on a loved one's face and suddenly forget our own problems and go to that person. We hear of a tragedy on the news, and our own petty concerns dissolve into compassion for the victims of the violence. This is the power of mercy. It pulls us out of ourselves, makes us forget ourselves, and it happens without much effort. But to receive this gift, the strength of mercy, we first need to find the courage to enter into the space — geographically, emotionally, spiritually — of those who are sick and suffering, whoever or wherever they may be.

By the way, we may think of the sick as just those in hospitals or stuck in a room at home because of a cold or flu. But let's not forget there are many other kinds of sickness that we may not typically think of as such. For instance, there are the sicknesses of addiction, depression, and extreme anxiety. In a certain sense, there's also the "sickness" of old age. Of course, these kinds of illness aren't contagious, but when someone is suffering from them, there's a temptation to avoid that person. Well, let's not pull away. Let's pray for the courage to go out of our comfort zones and comfort Christ in the sick.

One last point before we conclude this section: Let's comfort the sick by encouraging them not to waste their suffering. In other words, let's remind them — tactfully and without pulling away our compassion — of their invaluable ministry of offering up their suffering by joining it to the perfect and acceptable sacrifice of Christ on the Cross. This is often a much-needed reminder in our day. After all, we live in a world that tells the sick that their suffering is meaningless and that they should avoid it at all costs. But when the sick embrace their suffering out of love for God and others (joining it to Christ's suffering on the Cross), then their suffering has eternal value and can bear great fruit for the kingdom of God.

To illustrate this point, I'd like to briefly tell the story of one of the most remarkable people I've ever known: Fr. Mark Garrow, MIC.

Father Mark was the superior general of my religious community, meaning he was in charge of hundreds of Marian priests and brothers stationed throughout the world. After his demanding six-year term in Rome had ended, he was basically allowed to choose any assignment in the community. Surprisingly, instead of choosing an easy job where he could get some well-deserved rest, he chose one of the most difficult positions of all: novice master, which is to be in charge of the spiritual formation of the men who are preparing to make their first profession of vows. And something made this position especially difficult: I was one of his novices!

During that novitiate year, I got to know a man of deep faith, hard work, tender love, and incredible humility. For instance, instead of simply assigning us novices the usual menial tasks, which is part of novitiate formation, this former superior general took the lowliest jobs. I clearly remember seeing him on his hands and knees, diligently scrubbing the toilets and showers, and I vividly recall how he was always the first one to jump up to clear the tables and do the dishes. Also, he had a way of anticipating the needs of everyone in the community, noticing if someone was going through a difficult time and doing little things to cheer that person up.

Needless to say, Fr. Mark became a deeply loved father figure and model of holiness for every one of the eight men in our house of formation. We all cared about him very much, which made the next part particularly difficult.

One day, shortly after my novitiate, Fr. Mark came up to me in the library where I was studying and shared that he had just been diagnosed with tongue cancer. He said it was serious, asked for my prayers, and explained that he would be offering up the pain for all the men in formation. In other words, he was going to lovingly accept his suffering, unite it to Jesus on the Cross, and ask the Lord to bless us postulants, novices, and seminarians.

Father Mark endured months of radiation and chemo-therapy treatments, which unfortunately, made his cancer worse. During that difficult time, he could hardly talk, could only consume liquid, and the whole right side of his face became painfully swollen. Eventually, he had to remain in bed or in an easy chair from which he would offer Mass in a barely audible way.

Of course, all the guys in formation loved to attend this Mass with Fr. Mark in his room. I especially loved it, because I could see that as he said the words of consecration — "This is my body ... given up for you. ... This is the chalice of my blood ... poured out for you" — he was lovingly offering himself and his sufferings to Christ for all his spiritual sons in formation and for our little community. And his offering bore great fruit, especially after the cancer took its course.

Following Fr. Mark's death in 2007, all the men in formation in our community in the United States personally experienced the grace of his "offered up" sufferings — and then the boom happened. We quickly went from having less than 10 men in formation the year of Fr. Mark's passing to nearly 30 by 2013, and we believe this happened as a result of Fr. Mark lovingly accepting his suffering and uniting it to Christ on the Cross.

As he suffered, Fr. Mark himself believed his suffering had value and would bear fruit, and this was a great comfort to him. So, again, let's comfort the sick in our own lives by reminding them that they and their suffering have value and can bear great fruit for the kingdom.

Fr. Mark Garrow, MIC, with his spiritual sons, shortly before his death in 2007.

During the ongoing vocation boom, 2013.

CONTINUE THE STORY...

> To learn more about Fr. Mark Garrow, MIC, Marian vocations, and more, visit **MercyPages.org** and click "Continue the Story."

~ Action Items ~
'I Was Sick and You Visited Me'
[Check the box next to any of the action items below that you might actually be able to do.]

☐ I will not avoid the sick in my own family. Rather, I will comfort them by…

> ☐ Offering to go to the store to get them such things as medicine, soup, and popsicles.

> ☐ Visiting them frequently (provided it doesn't annoy them).

> ☐ Trying my best to be patient with them in their suffering.

> ☐ Having someone from the parish bring them Holy Communion, if they desire it.

> ☐ Encouraging them not to waste their sufferings by reminding them — tactfully and without pulling away my compassion — of their invaluable ministry of lovingly offering up their suffering by joining it to the perfect and acceptable sacrifice of Christ on the Cross.

> ☐ Other:_____

☐ I will make an effort to visit any sick friends who go to the hospital, provided they don't mind a visit.

☐ I will visit the local hospital to inquire into possibilities of hospital ministry.

> ☐ I'm particularly interested in helping those who are dying (hospice care). [Visit MercyPages.org under "I Was Sick and You Visited Me."]

> ☐ I'm particularly interested in bringing Holy Communion to the sick at the local hospital. [You would first need to speak with the pastor of your parish.]

> ☐ I'm particularly interested in _____

☐ I will call or visit more frequently any elderly friends or family members I may have.

→ Who? _____

→ When? _____

☐ I will visit the local home for the elderly to inquire into possibilities of ministering to them. I'm particularly interested in…

   ☐ Bringing them Holy Communion. [You would first need to speak with the pastor of your parish.]

   ☐ Simply visiting with them and listening to their stories.

   ☐ Sharing with them my talents of cooking, singing, magic tricks, or _____

☐ I will speak to the pastor at my parish to inquire into possibilities of ministering to any shut-ins from the parish. I'm particularly interested in…

   ☐ Helping them with their shopping.

   ☐ Bringing them Holy Communion.

   ☐ Cleaning or doing yard work for them.

   ☐ Visiting with them.

☐ I will speak to the pastor of my parish to inquire into opportunities to minister to any of the sick from the parish.

☐ I'm already a healthcare professional (doctor, nurse, etc.), and I will contact Healthcare Professionals for Divine Mercy to learn more about how I can better bring the grace of God's mercy into my patient care. [Visit MercyPages.org under "I Was Sick and You Visited Me."]

☐ I know someone who has an addiction, and I'm going to reach out to help that person.

   ☐ I will do research on the Internet about any addictions my friends or family have to see what kind of help is available. [Visit MercyPages.org under "I Was Sick and You Visited Me."]

CHAPTER FIVE

'I Was in Prison and You Came to Me'

This last Scriptural category covers one corporal and two spiritual works of mercy. The corporal work of mercy is "visit the imprisoned." The spiritual are "admonish sinners" and "pray for the living and the dead." Let's start with the corporal work of mercy.

VISIT THE IMPRISONED. I'd like to open this topic by first saying something about the patron saint of prisoners, St. Maximilian Kolbe.

Most people know St. Maximilian as the Polish priest who chose death in the Auschwitz prison camp to save the life of another. What they don't always realize is that St. Maximilian is also one of the greatest apostles of Marian consecration. He vigorously promoted this Marian devotion because his one desire in life was to give the greatest possible glory to God. (Hence the name "Maximilian," which means "the greatest.") With St. Louis de Montfort, he taught that a total consecration to Jesus through Mary is the "surest, easiest, shortest, and the most perfect" path to becoming a saint.[17] Believing that nothing is more important than sanctity, he completely dedicated himself to promoting this Marian way.

St. Maximilian Kolbe, patron saint of prisoners.

I write all this about St. Maximilian as a preface to another story. This one involves my friend Eric Mahl, about whom I wrote earlier.

As you may recall, Eric is the former football player who desired to serve the Lord, ended up at the National Shrine of The Divine Mercy in Stockbridge, and now runs our works of mercy programs. While these programs serve all those in need, Eric and I felt that the Lord was calling us to reach out to those in prison in a particular way. Eric's thought was this: "Yes, let's do it, but it can't just be to say hello. If we're going to do it, let's do it right. Let's help them to become saints, great saints, and quickly." In other words, he wanted to introduce the prisoners to total consecration to Jesus through Mary.

An opportunity for this ministry came when Eric was invited to participate in the first Hearts Afire Program at a federal prison. He said yes, because the first stage of the program involves a retreat in preparation for Marian consecration.

After arriving at the prison, Eric and the other volunteers were escorted by prison guards to the meeting space, where they waited for the inmates. When the men eventually filed in, they kept to themselves and didn't look very interested in participating in any program. To many of them, it was just an excuse to get out of their cells.

Knowing he would have to give a talk to this tough crowd, Eric turned to the Holy Spirit in prayer. As he did, a poignant scene from the movie *The Passion of the Christ* popped into his mind, which I'll describe now.

The scene follows Jesus' condemnation before the Sanhedrin and his brutal arrest in the courtyard of Caiaphas. It opens with Mary, the mother of Jesus, slowly, deliberately walking around the empty courtyard, like she's looking for something and straining to hear. Amid the flickering glow of wall torches, she suddenly crouches down and gently, tenderly, presses her cheek to the face of the stone floor. The camera moves downward, past the stones, and the viewer is taken further down into a dark and dreary dungeon where a bloody, shackled, and forlorn figure appears. It's Jesus, who, sensing his mother's presence, begins to gaze upward and is clearly comforted.

That's the scene Eric shared with a roomful of unhappy prisoners. Then, he told them the following:

> Just as Mary, the mother of Jesus wanted to be there for her Son in that dark prison, so also, Mary your mother wants to be here for you. We've come because we believe Mary sent us to you, her beloved sons. She hasn't forgotten you. She loves you, and she wants to come into this prison. She wants to heal your wounds and be a mother to you now. You just have to let her in. You just have to open up your hearts and let her come in. That's what the consecration we're starting today is all about.

With these and similar words, Eric invited the prisoners to give their lives to Jesus through Mary. Afterward and over the course of the retreat, he witnessed a transformation of those hardened men. The boredom and suspicion, the indifference and discouragement faded away and were replaced with excitement and joy. Week after week, their enthusiasm remained, regular Mass attendance exploded, and the anticipation for "consecration day" grew. In fact, toward the end of the retreat, the inmates' faces actually glowed with joy. Eric said, "They looked like little kids." Finally, at the conclusion of the 33 days of preparation, each one of them, Catholic and non-Catholic alike, devoutly gave his life to Jesus through Mary in a spirit of brotherhood that had been nearly non-existent before.

Amid the happiness and joy, one of the inmates even decided to change his name to "Max," having been so inspired by the portion of the retreat devoted to St. Maximilian Kolbe, whose name, again, means "the greatest." On hearing this news, Max's cellmate joked, "I thought I might have to clear some space in our cell to make room for his new name, but 'Max' was quick to clarify: 'I'm not the greatest,' he said, 'but my saint is!'"

"Max" (center left), making his consecration
to Jesus through Mary while in prison.

I tell this story of the first Hearts Afire Marian consecration program in a prison, because I believe Mary wants even
more of her forgotten children to entrust themselves to her
motherly care. If you ever decide to do prison ministry or are
involved in it now, I encourage you to introduce the inmates
to this Marian devotion. In other words, don't just go to visit
the prisoners. Rather, teach them how to become saints in
the "shortest, easiest, and surest" way. To help with this, for
as long as I am able, I will donate the Hearts Afire Program,
complete with its DVDs and study guides, to anyone who will
bring Jesus through Mary into a prison.[18]

Obviously, everyone can't do direct prison ministry like
Eric. If you can't, there's still something you can do to visit those
in prison. You can visit them with your prayers. Those in prison
are often forgotten and suffer so many things. I'm not even
going to get into the sad statistics regarding the shocking forms
of abuse that occur in prisons. Let's just say there's so much
brokenness and humiliation in prison, and therefore, inmates
are among the ones who are most deserving of the Lord's
mercy. Yes, in justice, they have to pay the price for their crimes
and do their time, but the Lord loves them most especially. For,
again, as Jesus tells us through St. Faustina, **"The greater the
sinner, the greater the right he has to My mercy."**[19]

Of course, I'm not saying everyone in prison is a big sinner. In fact, there are certainly prisoners who are innocent or deeply repentant and lead holy lives. And then, there are the millions of Christians who are persecuted for their faith. I'm thinking of those Christians who live in countries where there is little or no religious freedom. I'm thinking of the countless number of Christians who, even if they are not physically incarcerated, live in fear and psychological bondage to their fanatical countrymen.

Unfortunately, only rarely do we hear about these tormented brothers and sisters in Christ. Only rarely do we hear about the sufferings of this most persecuted religious group in the world. Only rarely do we hear about the brutal beatings, tortures, and hundreds of thousands of martyrdoms.

In an uncommon news piece detailing the persecution of Christians, an American journalist recounted his experience of meeting a large group of Christians fleeing some of the vicious persecution in the Middle East. He asked them, "What can be done?" The overwhelming response was not, "Give us money," "Give us guns," or "Give us asylum." Rather, time and again, the response was simply this: "Please do not forget us."

Another article on a website dedicated to covering the ongoing persecution of Christians tells a similar story, except that when the beleaguered Christians were asked what they needed, they answered, "Prayer." The article went on to explain the importance of such prayer:

> Prayer is the one thing that border guards and religious police cannot keep out. Prayer reaches the most remote villages and infiltrates the most inaccessible labor camps. Prayer changes things. The Church is shaken, bruised, grieving. But the Church is growing. The Church is enduring. The Church is alive. And the Church needs our prayer.[20]

May we never forget our persecuted brothers and sisters in Christ. May we learn of their stories, especially of those who live in countries such as North Korea, China, Somalia, Syria, Egypt, Iraq, Afghanistan, Saudi Arabia, Maldives, Pakistan, Iran, and Yemen. May we keep the persecuted Church in our prayers, always.

As many as 100,000 Christians are killed for their faith *every year*.

*A*DMONISH SINNERS. Why a majority Christian country such as the United States, with its massive political, economic, and military might, does not admonish the many countries that viciously persecute Christians and yet receive our monetary aid is beyond me. Unfortunately, apart from writing our representatives in Congress, it seems we can't do much more than pray. However, when it comes to the sins of our own families and communities, we do have influence. Indeed, we ourselves can and should, at times, admonish the sinners who are closest to home.

Alright, so we say to them, "Hey, you. Yes, you! STOP SINNING!" Right? Well, that's not quite what I mean here. The work of mercy "admonish sinners" is not a call to *demolish* sinners. That being said, it truly is an act of mercy to help free people from the prison of sin, to correct one another in charity — the key words being (a) "correct" and (b) "charity." Before we get to these two points, though, let me first say something about rules and sin.

Regarding Rules and Sin. Many people see sin as the fun stuff in life that the boring, self-righteous, hypocritical rule-makers nag them about to ruin their fun. They say, "Don't shove your rules down my throat, okay? I'm my own man. I'm free. I do what I want." The problem with this is that the rules are neither mine nor yours — they're God's. In other words, they're not man-made, they're God-made. So, ultimately, when it comes to morality, there's only one true Rule-Maker, and we choose either to follow his rules or not. (We commit sin when we choose not to follow them.)

In view of this point, I think the people who say, "Don't shove your rules down my throat" actually have at least one good point. I mean, nobody should force arbitrary, man-made morality down anyone's throats (or anything else, for that matter). That is, we have to be careful not to equate God's rules with our own rules, which can become a form of self-righteousness. An example of such behavior is when we judge as wrong some action that's not actually wrong or at least not as wrong as we think it is. Put differently, it's when we add our own ideas and personal preferences to the moral law and act as if such changes were Gospel truth.

You can sometimes see this form of self-righteousness in popular videos on the Internet, in books, and in periodicals that are put out by those who pontificate on their own self-styled morality as if they were the Supreme Lawgiver himself. They're the ones who read "Admonish the sinner" and begin to salivate. They seem to love to condemn others and think of themselves as mini-messiahs saving our corrupted world. Such people, if motivated by anger and hate, truly deserve the curses and condemnations that Jesus reserved for the scribes and the Pharisees — in fact, they would be modern-day Pharisees. May the Lord have mercy on them.

(1) 'Correct.' So, my first point is that if we're going to correct someone as an act of charity, let's make sure we're truly correct when we correct. How horrible it is to condemn someone or something that's not really evil or that may even

be good. How reprehensible it is to add unnecessary weight to people who are already bowed down by the weight of their own crosses. The Lord reserves his strongest words for those who do this, those who "bind heavy burdens, hard to bear, and lay them on men's shoulders" (Mt 23:4). Indeed, he doesn't hesitate to call such people "fools," "blind guides," and "hypocrites" while cursing them with "woes."

Still, the modern-day Pharisees do have a point — or an emotion at least. They're angry. They're upset. They're furious because things are really bad. And on this point, I think they're right: Morally speaking, things are pretty bad these days. However, I disagree with them that the solution is to indiscriminately unload on others with our morality bazookas and whip people up into a frenzy of rash judgment-making. I disagree with them that all the world's problems are the fault of uncourageous bishops, lukewarm priests, and hypocritical Catholics.

I rather agree with the eminent Catholic writer G.K. Chesterton who answered an interviewer's question, "What's wrong with the world?" by simply stating, "I am." In other words, I think each of us should say, "*I'm* the problem. If I were a saint, if I were more generous, less lazy, and less indifferent, things would certainly be different." Indeed, the modern crisis is primarily a dearth of saints, not the proliferation of sinners. The devil did confess, after all, to St. John Vianney, "If there were three men like you on this earth, my reign would collapse." Our first responsibility, then, is to strive to be one of those three.

So, the second point is that we should strive to be "correct" ourselves before we correct others. Sure, things are a mess, but each of us is a mess, too. Therefore, before we go around on a mission of correcting, we should first make sure our own house is in order. Now, this isn't an excuse to never correct anyone. But it is a warning that we should be careful of the hypocrisy that's quick to condemn when we ourselves do the very same things, or worse: "You hypocrite, first take the log out of your own eye, and then you will see clearly to take the speck out of your brother's eye" (Mt 7:5).

And what's the log that's often caught in our own eyes that makes it difficult to properly correct others? It's our failure to live one of the works of mercy we've already covered, "bear wrongs patiently." How often is our desire to correct others really just a temptation to sin against mercy, because we're too thin-skinned and morally weak ourselves to bear another's weakness? How often do we want to correct someone just because their actions are annoying to us, and the easiest route is to simply shut them down? I suspect that this is the more common danger than a lack of courage to correct.

Perhaps providentially, just this morning as I'm writing this book, I read in the Office of Readings an example of how the Church reminds us of this danger. In the second reading, Blessed Isaac of Stella, abbot, begins by asking why we care so little about each other's well-being that we are so unwilling to "bear one another's burdens" as St. Paul calls us to do. He asks:

> Why can I not patiently bear the weaknesses I see in my brother which, either out of necessity or because of physical or moral weakness, cannot be corrected? … Is it because I lack that virtue which suffers all things, is patient enough to bear all, and generous enough to love?
>
> This is indeed the law of Christ, who truly *bore our weakness* in his passion and carried our sorrows out of pity, loving those he carried and carrying those he loved. Whoever attacks a brother in need, or plots against him in his weakness of whatever sort, surely fulfills the devil's law and subjects himself to it. Let us then be compassionate toward one another, loving our brothers, bearing one another's weaknesses, yet ridding ourselves of our sins.
>
> The more any way of life sincerely strives for the love of God and the love of our neighbor for God's sake, the more acceptable it is to God … . For charity is the reason why anything should be done or left undone, changed or left unchanged; it

is the initial principle and the end to which all things should be directed.[21]

And so, the words of this good abbot bring us from one key word to another. They bring us from "correct," as in we need to correct ourselves first by learning to bear one another's burdens, to "charity," as in we need to strive to do everything, including correcting or not correcting, always with an eye to the tender light of charity.

(2) "Charity." What does it mean to correct "in charity?" Well, let's go back to our definition of sin as the breaking of God's rules. Now, God's rules, the Ten Commandments, are not meant to make us miserable.[22] They're not meant to ruin our fun. They're not meant to take away our freedom. Rather, they're meant to give us true freedom, peace, and joy. We may not always recognize this reality, but it's the reason God gave them. Trust me — better yet, trust him. (See Psalm 119.)

In our contemporary society, though, people don't always get this point. For instance, when they choose a lifestyle that clearly breaks God's law, they'll often respond, "Whatever, man. I am happy. I love my sin, and I don't need you and your God." What do we say then? How do we answer that? Sure, we can give them the statistics showing that those who choose such a life tend to not be happy, but that route may not work if the people are genuinely content living a life of sin. In fact, it's actually kind of silly to tell someone "you're not happy" when they insist that they are.

Alright, then, what do we say? Well, we can go the other route, the blunt route of St. Paul who said, "Do you not know that the unrighteous will not inherit the kingdom of God? Do not be deceived; neither the immoral, nor idolaters, nor adulterers, nor homosexuals, nor thieves, nor the greedy, nor drunkards, nor revilers, nor robbers will inherit the kingdom of God" (1 Cor 6:9). In other words, we can put the fear of hell in people. Or can we? Many people think hell doesn't even exist. It's little more than a joke or a children's fairy tale. Alright, so how do we admonish sinners who don't even believe in hell?

Well, I think the key is "in charity." In other words, we tell them about God's mercy, radiate his love, and remain patient. I'm not saying there aren't times for fire and brimstone. I'm not saying there aren't times for calling out hypocrisy, corruption, and evil. There are such times, but we need to be careful, because there's a lot of room for ego and anger and rash judgment along that route, and it should never be our "go to move." Of course, Jesus himself used the "tough love move," but interestingly enough, it was rare and almost always reserved for the Pharisees. For the common sinners, he almost always practiced a gentle, patient love. He ate with them, hung out with them, and attracted them to himself with his truth and mercy.

Alright, but these things are tricky. Wouldn't it be helpful to have a contemporary example that speaks to our modern context, an example of one who admonishes the sinner, "in charity"? Sure would be helpful, and the Lord has provided such an example in our present Pope, Francis. He seems to get it. He "admonishes the sinner" in a way that doesn't break the broken reed. And he's been wildly successful. Throughout the world, there are reports of the "Francis effect," which refers to the massive number of fallen-away Catholics and the even greater number of non-Catholics who are giving the Church a second look.

A great "Mercy Pope."

While Pope Francis has certainly not watered down the teaching of the Church and while he has clearly been tough on such things as corruption and clericalism, his emphasis has consistently been on mercy. For example, his view of the Church as that of "a field hospital after battle" seems inspired by the wisdom of mercy. He himself explains its simple logic:

> It is useless to ask a seriously injured person if he has high cholesterol and about the level of his blood sugars! You have to heal his wounds. Then we can talk about everything else. Heal the wounds, heal the wounds.[23]

People are deeply wounded in the modern world, and Pope Francis recognizes that they need the medicine of mercy and not a scold. "[T]he thing the Church needs most today is the ability to heal wounds and to warm the hearts of the faithful. … [T]he ministers of the Church must be ministers of mercy above all."[24]

As the Francis effect shows, this mercy approach is working, which shouldn't surprise us if we consider what Jesus told St. Faustina regarding priests who take such an approach:

> **Tell My priests that hardened sinners will repent on hearing their words when they speak about My unfathomable mercy, about the compassion I have for them in My Heart. To priests who proclaim and extol My mercy, I will give wondrous power; I will anoint their words and touch the hearts of those to whom they will speak.[25]**

This power of mercy worked on me. I clearly remember listening to the simultaneous translation of Pope Francis's first public homily, and it melted my heart. It moved me like no other papal homily. It revealed the face of a God whom people can fall in love with. And while hardened sinners who may have heard it might still choose their sins and say, "I don't need your morality!" If they truly listened, they'd find it hard to say, "I don't need your God." Why? Because the words of the homily wipe away a lie and plant a seed. The lie: God is a mean, petty tyrant who just wants to ruin our fun. The seed: Ours is a God of patience, love, and mercy. He's demanding, for sure — he requires us to give up our sins — but he's demanding because he loves us, and whether or not we give up our sins doesn't change his love. Also, as the Pope made clear, this love of God that pursues us is patient, understanding, and never gives up on us.

Let's close this section by reflecting on the gentle, merciful way that Pope Francis admonishes the sinner and reveals the true face of God in his first public homily:

> I think we too are the people who, on the one hand want to listen to Jesus, but on the other hand, at times, like to find a stick to beat others with, to condemn others. And Jesus has this message for us: mercy. I think — and I say it with humility — that this is the Lord's most powerful message: mercy. It was he himself who said: "I did not come for the righteous." The righteous justify themselves. [To them, I say,] "Go on, then, even if you can do it, I cannot!" But they believe they can. [Yet, Jesus said,] "I came for sinners" (Mk 2:17).
>
> Think of the gossip after the call of Matthew: He associates with sinners! (See Mk 2:16.) He comes for us, when we recognize that we are sinners. But if we are like the Pharisee, before the altar, who said: "I thank you, Lord, that I am not like other men, and especially not like the one at the door, like that publican" (see Lk 18:11-12), then we do not know the Lord's heart, and we will never have the joy of experiencing this mercy!
>
> It is not easy to entrust oneself to God's mercy, because it is an abyss beyond our comprehension. But we must! "Oh, Father, if you knew my life, you would not say that to me!" "Why, what have you

done?" "Oh, I am a great sinner!" "All the better! Go to Jesus: he likes you to tell him these things!" He forgets, he has a very special capacity for forgetting. He forgets, he kisses you, he embraces you and he simply says to you: "Neither do I condemn you; go, and sin no more" (Jn 8:11). That is the only advice he gives you. After a month, if we are in the same situation ... Let us go back to the Lord. The Lord never tires of forgiving: never! It is we who tire of asking his forgiveness. Let us ask for the grace not to tire of asking forgiveness, because he never tires of forgiving. Let us ask for this grace.[26]

*P*RAY FOR THE LIVING AND THE DEAD. Remember the Three Degrees of Mercy that Jesus taught St. Faustina? They were mercy in deed, word, and prayer. Regarding the last point, prayer, you may recall St. Faustina's comment, "If I cannot show mercy by deeds, I can always do so by prayer. My prayer reaches out even there where I cannot reach out physically."[27] How beautiful prayer is! We can always be putting mercy into action, even from far away, because we can always pray.

I decided to save prayer for last because it is the one work of mercy that we can always do at any time and in any place, and it covers all the other works of mercy. For again, "If I cannot show mercy by deeds," says St. Faustina, "I can always do so by prayer." What does this mean in light of what we've already covered? It means we can always pray *for the hungry* that they will have enough food to eat; we can always pray *for those who feel alone and unwelcomed,* "the stranger," that they will experience the warmth of Christ's love; we can always pray *for the naked*, that they will be clothed; we can always pray *for the sick*, that they will be cared for and comforted; we can always pray *for those in prison*, that Christ will go to them with his grace and mercy.

Another reason why I saved this work of mercy for now is that it applies so well to our present Scriptural category, "visit those in prison."

As you recall, praying for prisoners is often the only thing we can do to help them. In fact, among all the five groups we've covered — the hungry, the stranger, the naked, the sick, and those in prison — it's safe to say that the most inaccessible group is almost always the imprisoned. Therefore, now is the perfect time to talk about prayer. And it's appropriate for two more reasons.

First, as we'll learn later in this section, probably the most important group of people to pray for is *unrepentant sinners* (those who are deeply in the bondage, the "prison," of sin). Second, purgatory, which we cover under our present topic because it includes praying for "the dead," is very much like prison. In fact, Scripture itself describes purgatory as a prison. (See Mt 5:22-26; Lk 12:59-58.)[28] Well, this side of eternity, the *only* way we can visit the souls imprisoned in purgatory is through prayer.

Alright, so that helps explain why we're treating prayer here. And now, let's dive into this topic by looking more closely at prayer itself — specifically, at prayer as an act of mercy.

There are all types of prayer. For instance, there's adoration, contrition, praise, and thanksgiving. The prayer of mercy is called *intercession*, or prayer for the needs of others. So, how do we pray for others as an act of mercy? Well, let me put it this way: *Any* prayer for someone who is suffering or in need is a prayer of mercy. Of course, that's pretty general. Okay, then, to be more specific, I'd like to focus on what's probably the most popular "mercy prayer" and certainly one of the most effective: the Chaplet of Divine Mercy. After we learn about this chaplet, let's determine our "prayer priorities" — in other words, let's find out who is most in need of our prayers.

(1) *The Chaplet of Divine Mercy.* The Chaplet of Divine Mercy is prayed on ordinary rosary beads, and as I already mentioned, it's pretty popular today, perhaps because it only takes about seven minutes to pray. (To learn how to pray it, see Appendix Two.)

I think a bigger reason why the chaplet is so popular is that it's such an incredibly powerful prayer. Why is it so powerful? Because it draws its strength from the holiest and mightiest prayer there is: the Mass. In other words, the Chaplet of Divine Mercy is a kind of extension of the prayer of the Mass. In fact, it's a kind of extension of what I call the "supercharged moment of the Mass." Here's what I mean: It's an extension of that moment when the priest at the altar takes the Body and Blood of Christ into his hands and offers it up to the Father with these words:

> Through him, and with him, and in him, O God, almighty Father, in the unity of the Holy Spirit, all glory and honor is yours forever and ever. Amen.

That's supercharged because, at the Mass, Jesus is giving himself Body, Blood, Soul, and Divinity into our hands: literally, in the hands of the priest and spiritually, in the hands of all the lay faithful who are uniting their own sacrifices to the offering of the priest at the altar. Together, each in his own way, we offer Jesus' infinite sacrifice of love to the Father. That's the power of the Mass. It's Jesus' own sacrifice of love in our hands, held up to the Father, and the Father can't resist such a perfect sacrifice of love. It really is the perfect prayer.

Now, the chaplet is like an extension of that moment of the Mass, because on the "Our Father" beads of the rosary, we pray, "Eternal Father, I offer You the Body and Blood, Soul and Divinity of Your dearly beloved Son, our Lord Jesus Christ …[for what?] … in atonement for our sins and those of [what? … my family? … my city? ... no, not just that …] *the whole world*." So, it's a bold prayer: It's for the whole world! And it can be bold because it relies on infinite merits: Christ's infinite sacrifice of love on the Cross. Make sure, then, that when you pray the chaplet, you spiritually unite your prayers to all the Masses being offered in the world at that time.[29]

Alright, so that explains the "Our Father" beads. Now to the "Hail Marys."

On each "Hail Mary" bead, we pray, "For the sake of His sorrowful Passion, have mercy on us and on the whole world." In other words, as we're holding up to the Father his Son's infinite sacrifice of love, we keep repeating: "Mercy, mercy, mercy." More specifically, we keep praying, "Have mercy on us and on the whole world." And this is powerful. Believe me. I've seen its power. I've heard the testimonies. And you know who it's most powerful for? The dying. Our Heavenly Father said to St. Faustina:

When this chaplet is said by the bedside of a dying person ... unfathomable mercy envelops the soul, and the very depths of My tender mercy are moved for the sake of the sorrowful Passion of My Son.[30]

Also, Jesus made several comforting promises to those who pray the chaplet:

Say unceasingly the chaplet that I have taught you. Whoever will recite it will receive great mercy at the hour of death. ... Even if there were a sinner most hardened, if he were to recite this chaplet only once, he would receive grace from My infinite mercy.[31]

The souls that say this chaplet will be embraced by My mercy during their lifetime and especially at the hour of their death.[32]

Oh, what great graces I will grant to souls who say this chaplet; the very depths of My tender mercy are stirred for the sake of those who say the chaplet.[33]

My daughter, encourage souls to say the chaplet which I have given to you. It pleases Me to grant everything they ask of Me by saying the chaplet.

When hardened sinners say it, I will fill their souls with peace, and the hour of their death will be a happy one.[34]

"Say unceasingly the chaplet."

(2) Unrepentant Sinners, Especially Those Who Are Dying. These words from the *Diary of St. Faustina* are certainly an encouragement to pray the Chaplet of Divine Mercy, especially for the dying and for sinners. But why does Jesus emphasize praying for these two groups of people? We'll get a clue from some other *Diary* passages where Jesus asks St. Faustina to pray for these groups. Regarding sinners, he says:

Do not grow weary of praying for sinners. You know what a burden their souls are to My Heart. Relieve My deathly sorrow; dispense My mercy.[35]

The loss of each soul plunges Me into mortal sadness. You always console Me when you pray for sinners. The prayer most pleasing to Me is prayer for the conversion of sinners. Know, My daughter, that this prayer is always heard and answered.[36]

And regarding the dying, Jesus tells Faustina:

Pray as much as you can for the dying. By your entreaties, obtain for them trust in My mercy, because they have most need of trust, and have it the least. Be assured that the grace of eternal salvation for certain souls in their final moment depends on your prayer. You know the whole abyss of My mercy, so draw upon it for yourself and especially for poor sinners.[37]

So, why does Jesus put such an emphasis on praying for sinners and the dying? Because of hell. Again, as he said to St. Faustina, **"The loss of each soul plunges me into mortal sadness."** Obviously, Jesus does not want anyone to go to hell. But the reality is, people will go to hell if they die in mortal sin.[38] So, the people in greatest danger of hell are those in a state of mortal sin, especially those who are dying, **"They have the most need of trust, and have it the least."** Jesus wants us to pray for such people, that they will turn away from sin and trust in his mercy. This is a great act of mercy: saving souls from the prison of hell, from which there is no escape! Jesus wants us to help him save them. Consider his words to St. Faustina and what happened next:

My daughter, help Me to save souls. You will go to a dying sinner, and you will continue to recite the chaplet, and in this way you will obtain for him trust in My mercy, for he is already in despair.

Suddenly, I found myself in a strange cottage where an elderly man was dying amidst great torments. All about the bed was a multitude of demons and the family, who were crying. When I began to pray [the chaplet], the spirits of darkness fled, with hissing and threats directed at me. The soul became calm and, filled with trust, rested in the Lord.

At the same moment, I found myself again in my own room. How this happens ... I do not know.[39]

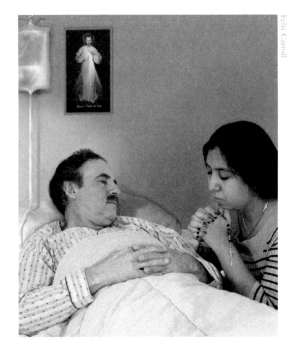

"Pray as much as you can for the dying."

When we pray the chaplet for the dying, we probably won't be mystically transported as St. Faustina was in the above account, but the reality is the same, and the stakes are just as high. Prayers for the conversion of hardened sinners, especially those who are dying, are most pleasing to Jesus and save souls. So, let's pray for them and remember Jesus' sobering words, **"Be assured that the grace of eternal salvation for certain souls in their final moment depends on your prayers."** See what responsibility we have!

Oh, but what about if we're too late? What about those who have already died? Can we pray for them as well? According to St. Padre Pio, we can pray for them because God is outside of time and can apply our prayers "now" back "then."[40] Also, according to the Church herself and the testimony of the saints, we need not lose hope for those who commit suicide. We can and should pray for them, too. (To read the reasons, see this endnote.[41])

(3) *The Souls in Purgatory.* Again, according to the *Diary of St. Faustina*, the most important group to pray for is unrepentant sinners in the state of mortal sin, especially those who are dying. But the Lord also encourages Faustina to pray for the souls in purgatory. Before we see why it's so important to pray for them, let's first review what purgatory is.

According to the *Catechism of the Catholic Church*, purgatory, or "the final purification," is for all those who die "in God's grace and friendship" but who are "still imperfectly purified." Such people will surely make it to heaven, but before they do, they will have to "undergo purification." What is this purification? The tradition of the Church, basing itself on Sacred Scripture, describes it as a "cleansing fire."[42] And what does it feel like? Well, we know this much: It's *painful.* And as for the worst of it, we have the following testimony from St. Faustina, who was mystically transported to purgatory:

> I saw my Guardian Angel, who ordered me to follow him. In a moment I was in a misty place full of fire in which there was a great crowd of suffering souls. They were praying fervently, but to no avail, for themselves; only we can come to their aid. The flames which were burning them did not touch me at all. My Guardian Angel did not leave me for an instant. I asked these souls what their greatest suffering was. They answered me in one voice that their greatest torment was longing for God. I saw Our Lady visiting the souls in Purgatory. The souls call her "The Star of the Sea." She brings them refreshment. I wanted to talk with them some more, but my Guardian Angel beckoned me to leave. We went out of that prison of suffering. [And I heard an interior voice] which said, **My mercy does not want this, but justice demands it.** Since that time, I am in closer communion with the suffering souls.[43]

What an amazing testimony! It not only tells us about the worst pain of purgatory, but it also raises several other important points about this "prison of suffering." Let's look at each point in turn so as to better appreciate why we should have mercy on the souls in purgatory.

First, "there was a great crowd." Many mystics testify that there's a huge number of souls in purgatory, perhaps more souls than there are people on earth! In that case, the need is massive, considering the sheer quantity of suffering souls.

Second, the souls in Faustina's experience were praying "fervently" for themselves "but to no avail." As Faustina rightly says, "Only we can come to their aid." In other words, the poor souls can't pray for themselves — they are completely at our mercy! And they certainly need our help.

Third, Faustina describes purgatory, as does Sacred Scripture, as a "prison." So, again, praying for the souls in purgatory is a true act of mercy, a way of visiting those in prison. This is pretty amazing when you think about it. Prayer for the hungry truly and most definitely helps, but it doesn't actually feed the hungry; prayer for the stranger truly helps, but it doesn't actually welcome the stranger; prayer for those without adequate clothing truly helps, but it doesn't actually clothe them; prayer for the sick truly helps, but it doesn't directly comfort the sick; prayer for those in prison truly helps, but it isn't the same as actually visiting them; *but prayer and sacrifice for those in the prison of purgatory directly and immediately consoles them.* The prayer itself is also the action. Our prayers actually visit them with grace!

Fourth, Jesus says, **"My mercy does not want this"** — so even Jesus doesn't want souls to have to suffer in purgatory. Nevertheless, he must be true to his word, which says that no taint, no sin, no unclean thing can enter into heaven, which is the full presence of God, who is all good and all holy. (See Rev 21:27.) So, to enter heaven, most souls must first be purified, even though Jesus himself longs for the souls in purgatory to be with him. In view of this, it's clear that we fulfill his desire, we please the Lord, when we pray for the souls in purgatory and thereby bring them closer to him. (I'm sure this also pleases his mother, the "Star of the Sea.")

St. Faustina visits purgatory with her Guardian Angel and Mary.

Fifth, the souls in purgatory also long to be with Jesus. In fact, according to St. Faustina, this longing is their greatest suffering. No wonder purgatory is expressed as a fire. Yes, the fire of longing! People who have lost a very dear loved one understand something of this longing. The grief, the heart-ache, the yearning to see the beloved again, the desire to die — all this is but a faint shadow of the pain of purgatory. Why? Because the souls in purgatory understand much better than we do the beauty and goodness and love of God, and they also know that it is their own sinfulness that keeps them from him. So, as they burn with desire to see the Lord, they also have to face the reality that their separation from him is their own fault. Their pangs of conscience and pain from self-rebuke must be unbearable. We can't imagine the intensity of the remorse, the desperation, the longing. Their one consolation is our prayers and to know it will end and that they will eventually see the face of God — but when? In many ways, that part is up to us.

Let's continue with this last point: *It's up to us.*

Imagine the worst prison cell in the world. It's stuffy, dark, and miserable. A man is stuck there and has no idea of when he can get out.

You know he's in there. In fact, his cell is right next to your bedroom, in your house. Every day, you pass by his locked room as you go about your business. Meanwhile, the guy inside is dying with longing to get out. It's all he thinks about. He doesn't eat, sleep, or drink. He's just there, 24 hours a day, burning with desire to be out of there, to get back to his wife and children, whom he dearly misses.

Now, as you walk by his door, he can hear the clanging of the keys on your keychain. One of those keys, which you carry with you every day, unlocks his cell door. You just have to take the time to stop, pull out the key, and unlock the door. If you do this, the prisoner will walk out of his cell a free man. And once he gets out, he won't have to go to a halfway house. Rather, his whole family is eagerly waiting for him right inside your living room. He wants to see them so badly, and all you have to do is take out that key and open the door for him. It's up to you. It's totally up to you. He's completely at your mercy.

Now, let's say you're so gracious as to take the brief time out of your day to open the door for him. Can you imagine that guy's gratitude? He'd do anything for you! Oh, and did I mention that his brother is your boss? Yeah, and when you let him out, he's going to embrace his brother and tell him all about how generous you were for letting him out and all about how he would have been stuck in that horrible place for God knows how long had you not come to help him. Of course, he's going to tell his brother to help you in a thousand different ways. Night and day, he's going to plead with his brother until he rewards you.

I think you get the idea. It's *so easy* to help the souls suffering in purgatory, and it makes *a huge* difference to them. I can't think of anything else that takes such little effort, yet immediately means so much to someone else. Perhaps this is why some saints have said that prayer for the souls in purgatory is one of the greatest acts of mercy.

Now, if this mercy aspect isn't enough to inspire us to pray for the poor souls regularly, maybe the part about the reward of their prayers will. I mean, just as we cannot comprehend the suffering of the souls in purgatory, neither can we fully gauge their generosity. The souls that your efforts release from purgatory (or that at least bring them consolation) will be *eternally* grateful. From heaven, right before the face of God, night and day, they'll pray for you and your family. And these prayers will be powerful. Praying for the souls in purgatory is one of the best deals going!

Alright, great. So whether we do it simply from the goodness of our hearts or because we also like the idea of having permanent friends in high places who can pull spiritual strings for us — let's just do it. (I hope it will be the former and not the latter reason.) Okay, but how do we pray for the souls in purgatory?

Praying for the souls in purgatory can be as simple as lovingly reciting one "Hail Mary" for them. And while that is certainly effective, I'd like to suggest five ways of praying for the Poor Souls, the "big five," that I believe are the most effective for helping to release them from the prison of purgatory.

First, *have a Mass said for them.* There is no more powerful prayer for the deceased than the Holy Sacrifice of the Mass. And while it's especially efficacious to pray for the repose of a soul while at Mass and to offer one's communion for him, having a Mass itself offered for one of the deceased is the most powerful of all. It could only get better if we were to have *several* Masses said for him.[44] See your local parish secretary about having a Mass said or contact the Marian Fathers.[45]

Second, *enroll the deceased in a spiritual benefit society.*
Certain religious congregations have been given special permission from the Holy See to extend their spiritual benefits to
those who are officially enrolled in their registers. This means
that those enrolled can continually share in the spiritual merits
of the Masses, prayers, sacrifices, and good works of a given
congregation. One of the main reasons why my own congregation, the Marian Fathers of the Immaculate Conception, was
founded, was to give relief to the souls suffering in purgatory.
For this reason, each Marian is required to offer up prayers
and sacrifices for the deceased. Having heard of our mission,
hundreds of thousands of people have enrolled their deceased
loved ones in our spiritual benefit society, called the Association
of Marian Helpers.

Third, offer an *indulgence for the deceased.* Now, bear with
me here. This point will take a bit more explaining than the
others, but it covers some very valuable information.

The *Catechism*'s teaching about indulgences is as follows:

> An indulgence is a remission before God of the
> temporal punishment due to sins whose guilt has
> already been forgiven, which the faithful Christian
> who is duly disposed gains under certain prescribed
> conditions through the action of the Church which,
> as the minister of redemption, dispenses and applies
> with authority the treasury of the satisfactions of
> Christ and the saints.[46]

Now let's look at the main points. First, an indulgence
is a "remission before God of the temporal punishment" due
to sin. The key words here are "temporal punishment," which
refer to the consequences of sin that are *not* removed even after
we repent and are forgiven by God. (Eternal punishment, the
punishment of hell, *is* removed by such forgiveness — ordinarily
through the Sacrament of Confession.)

To better understand what temporal punishment is,
imagine a situation where a parent forgives his repentant child

for stealing and eating one of the donuts that are sold after Sunday Mass at their parish. Of course, the relationship is healed by the repentance and forgiveness, but the child still needs to pay for the stolen donut. That requirement to pay is like temporal punishment, which we pay in the following ways: in this life, through penance, good works, and indulgences, and in the next life, through the suffering of purgatory. (The testimony of the mystics is that it is *much* easier to pay the price in this life than in the next.)

Thanks be to God, through indulgences, the Church helps us to reduce or completely remove our temporal punishment *relatively easily* in this life. (In terms of the above example, this would be like a situation where the parent pays for the stolen donut on behalf of the child in exchange for some simple chores at home.) And the Church can offer such a help, because it has the authority to "dispense and apply" the "satisfactions" of Christ and the saints. In other words, there's a storehouse of grace that comes from the suffering of Christ and his members that the Church can freely distribute to help us "pay off" our temporal punishment, provided we meet "certain prescribed conditions" and are "duly disposed."

What are these conditions and dispositions? Well, it depends on what type of indulgence we're looking for. For a partial indulgence, which means that some but not all of the temporal punishment due to sin is removed, we just need to be in the state of grace and perform the indulgenced act with the intention of receiving the indulgence. To receive a plenary indulgence, which means *all* of our temporal punishment is removed, there are six conditions:

- Be in the *state of grace*;
- Perform the *indulgenced act* with the intention of receiving the indulgence;
- *Go to confession* within "about 20 days" of performing the indulgenced act;
- *Receive the Eucharist* within about 20 days of the act;

- *Pray for the intentions of the Pope,* (for example, recite an "Our Father" and "Hail Mary"); and

- Have the interior disposition of *complete detachment from sin,* including venial sin (this is the tough one).

After giving this list of six conditions, I can't help but add a "super seventh," which comes to us from St. Thérèse of Lisieux, who writes, "The principal plenary indulgence, and one which everyone may obtain without the customary conditions, is the indulgence of *charity which covers a multitude of sins.*"[47] Amen.

Also, a "super eighth" happens to be the eighth day of Easter, Divine Mercy Sunday, which we learned about earlier. Remember the "special grace" that was likened to a "second Baptism"? Well, as we already read, Jesus promises us through St. Faustina that if we receive Holy Communion in the state of grace on that day, go to confession (at least sometime during Lent), and intend to receive this promised grace, then we will get a totally clean slate with all temporal punishment removed.[48] Not too shabby!

Now, here are a couple of other important things about indulgences. First, there's no limit to how many partial indulgences you can obtain in a day, but we can only get one plenary indulgence per day. Second, indulgences can be applied to either oneself or to the souls of the deceased, but they can't be applied to other living people.

Okay, that last point is the big one for our topic: You can get one soul out of his purgatorial prison, guaranteed, if you choose to apply your plenary indulgence to him. Now, the catch is the disposition of "complete detachment from sin, including venial." If you have that, then you can get a plenary indulgence every day, under the normal conditions. If you're attached to sin, though, then at least you can still get a partial indulgence.

Alright, now, before moving on to the next point, there may be one lingering question: Which acts, under the normal conditions, allow us to obtain a plenary indulgence? In her generosity, the Church offers such an indulgence for many different acts. Here are some of the most common ones:

- *Read Sacred Scripture* for at least one half hour.

- *Pray the Rosary* (five decades) out loud and continuously in a church or public oratory or in a family group, religious community, or pious association.

- *Pray the Stations of the Cross* before legitimately erected stations, such as in a church or at a shrine.

- *Adore Jesus in the Most Blessed Sacrament* for at least one half hour.

- *Pray the Prayer Before a Crucifix* on any Friday of Lent after receiving Holy Communion.[49]

Fourth, *offer sufferings for them*. We all suffer. We all have a cross to carry, daily. The important thing is that we not waste our sufferings. We don't waste them when we unite them to the sufferings of Christ with love and offer them to relieve the suffering of the souls in purgatory. We can also actively choose penances to offer for them, such as fasting.

Fifth, *pray the Chaplet of Divine Mercy for them*. We've already learned how powerful the chaplet is, so this is a given. But here I would add that if you want to offer your chaplet for the souls in purgatory, the eighth day of the Divine Mercy Novena has a beautiful reflection and prayer. (See pages 180-181.)

CONTINUE THE STORY...

> *To learn more about "Max" the prisoner, the Marians' prison ministry, Pope Francis's witness to mercy, the souls in purgatory, and more, visit* **MercyPages.org** *and click "Continue the Story."*

~ Action Items ~
'I Was in Prison and You Came to Me'
[Check the box next to any of the action items below that you might actually be able to do.]

Visit the Imprisoned…

☐ I will visit those in prison.

> ☐ I will contact the diocese or local prison chaplain to find out of any existing prison ministry.

> ☐ If I do begin ministry in a prison, I will try to introduce the Hearts Afire Program, starting with the *33 Days to Morning Glory* consecration preparation.

> ☐ If I'm allowed to start the Marian consecration program there, I will contact the Marians at 1-877-200-4277 or HAPP@marian.org for more information on how to get my free materials (while supplies last).

☐ In light of the Church's teaching on the death penalty (see *Catechism*, 2267), I will pray for an end to any and all unnecessary state execution of prisoners. [Visit MercyPages. org under "Visit the Imprisoned."]

☐ I will pray for those in prison, that they may be visited by the grace and mercy of Christ and grow in holiness.

☐ I will pray for the victims of crime, especially those who have suffered violence or who have lost a loved one, knowing that they often live in prisons of their own.

☐ I will remember and pray for the persecuted Church.

> ☐ I will do research on the Internet to learn more about the often hidden suffering of my persecuted brothers and sisters in Christ. [Visit MercyPages.org under "Visit the Imprisoned."]

> ☐ As I learn about their plight, I will tell others so to as to inspire them to remember and pray for these, my persecuted brothers and sisters.

Admonish Sinners…

☐ I will bear the weaknesses of others and not be too quick to correct them. I will strive to attract them to Christ by reflecting his love and mercy.

☐ When my neighbor is in need of correction, I will ask for the courage and grace to do it with love and mercy, and thereby reflect the true face of God.

☐ I will invite friends, family, and others to join me in going to the Sacrament of Confession.

  → Who? _____

Pray for the Living and the Dead…

☐ I will pray the Chaplet of Divine Mercy. [See Appendix Two.]

  → How often? _____

  → When?

    ☐ At 3:00 p.m. (the "Hour of Mercy").

    ☐ Another time: _____

☐ As an ongoing novena, I will include the Novena to Divine Mercy when I pray the Chaplet. [See Appendix Two.]

☐ I will pray for those in need, especially *for the hungry*, that they will have enough food to eat; *for those who feel alone and unwelcomed*, "the stranger," that they will experience the warmth of Christ's love; *for the naked*, that they will be clothed; *for the sick*, that they will be cared for and comforted; *for those in prison*, that Christ will go to them with his grace and mercy.

    ☐ I will remember them when I pray the Chaplet of Divine Mercy.

    ☐ I will remember them when I pray … _____

    _____

☐ I will consecrate myself to Jesus through Mary, so Mary can offer the grace of my prayers and sacrifices to God for me, especially for these intentions.

→ Which consecration?

☐ *33 Days to Morning Glory*

☐ Other: _____

☐ If I am already consecrated, I will speak to Mary about my desire to pray for these intentions, and I will trust that she will be mindful of them on my behalf. I will still pray for them explicitly when I can and when I feel moved to do so.

☐ I will pray most especially for unrepentant sinners, particularly for those who are dying.

☐ I will remember them when I pray the Chaplet of Divine Mercy.

☐ I will remember them when I pray ... _____

_____

☐ I will make sacrifices for the conversion of sinners.

→ What sacrifice(s)? _____

☐ I will consecrate myself to Jesus through Mary, so Mary can offer the grace of my prayers and sacrifices to God for me, especially for this intention of mercy for unrepentant sinners.

☐ If I am already consecrated, I will speak to Mary about these desires in my heart to pray for this intention, and I will trust that she will be mindful of it on my behalf. And I will still pray for it explicitly when I can and when I feel moved to do so.

☐ I will strive to help the souls in purgatory. I will do so by...

☐ Having Mass(es) said for them.

→ For whom? _____

→ At what parish or through which religious community?

_____

[Recommendation: Visit PrayforSouls.org or call 1-800-462-7426 to have a Marian priest offer a Mass.]

☐ Enrolling the deceased in the Association of Marian Helpers. [For more information, visit Prayforsouls.org or call 1-800-462-7426.]

    → Which deceased loved ones? _____

    _____

    _____

☐ Gaining indulgences for them.

    → Partial or plenary? _____

    → By doing what indulgenced act(s)? _____

    _____

    → How often? _____

☐ Offering some of my suffering and sacrifices for them.

☐ Remembering them when I pray the Chaplet of Divine Mercy.

    ☐ I will also pray the prayer from the eighth day of the Divine Mercy Novena. [See Appendix Two.]

☐ Remembering them when I pray the Rosary.

☐ Making the consecration to Jesus through Mary, if I'm not already consecrated. I will do this so Mary can remember to offer the grace of my prayers and sacrifices for me, especially for this intention of mercy for the souls in purgatory.

    ☐ If I am already consecrated, I will speak to Mary about these desires in my heart to pray for this intention, and I will trust that she will be mindful of it on my behalf. And I will still pray for it explicitly when I can and when I feel moved to do so.

CHAPTER SIX
Almsgiving

Why a separate chapter on almsgiving? As I mentioned earlier, it's a special work of mercy that, like prayer, covers all five of the Scriptural categories. In other words, just as we can pray for the hungry, the stranger, the naked, the sick, and those in prison, so also, we can financially support ministries that reach out to those in need. Therefore, St. Faustina's beautiful words about prayer that we read earlier also, in some sense, apply to almsgiving. ("If I cannot show mercy by deeds, I can always do so by prayer. My prayer reaches out even there where I cannot reach out physically.") Indeed, our financial support reaches out even where we cannot reach out physically.

Perhaps it's this special quality of almsgiving that inspired the place of honor the *Catechism* gives it in its section on the works of mercy, which we read earlier. Recall that after simply mentioning the other works of mercy, the *Catechism* says, "Among all these, giving alms to the poor is one of the chief witnesses to fraternal charity: it is also a work of justice pleasing to God."[50]

Okay, so almsgiving is something special, but I'd add that it also has to be done right. Just recently, I had a conversation that helps to illustrate what I mean.

The person I spoke with is one of the largest donors to my community's seminarian program. During the conversation, I thanked him for his support, saying it means so much to us right now. (Presently, we have 30 men in formation in the U.S. and only 23 active priests!) He looked at me as if he couldn't accept my thanks and explained, "You know, I'm not really being so generous. I give from my surplus, not from my need. It doesn't hurt me to give." His words struck me. Of course, they didn't change my gratitude to him for the important assistance he was giving us, but it did put things into a Gospel-centered perspective, where it's not so much about how much we give but rather *about how much it costs us to give*:

> And [Jesus] sat down opposite the treasury, and watched the multitude putting money into the

treasury. Many rich people put in large sums. And a poor widow came, and put in two copper coins, which make a penny. And he called his disciples to him, and said to them, "Truly, I say to you, this poor widow has put in more than all those who are contributing to the treasury. For they all contributed out of their abundance; but she out of her poverty has put in everything she had, her whole living" (Mk 12:41).

One of the most gripping parts of this passage, at least for me, is how Jesus sat down "and watched." Yes, he's watching us. He who was rich and became poor that we might become rich (see 2 Cor 8:9) looks to see if we also will be generous with him and with his people. But it's not so much about the amount we give. Rather, it's about our trust and the nature of our sacrifice. Does it come from our need or from our abundance?

In his 2014 letter to prepare the Church for Lent, Pope Francis emphasizes and develops this idea:

Dear brothers and sisters, may this Lenten season find the whole Church ready to bear witness to all those who live in material, moral, and spiritual destitution the Gospel message of the merciful love of God our Father, who is ready to embrace everyone in Christ. We can do this to the extent that we imitate Christ who became poor and enriched us by his poverty. Lent is a fitting time for self-denial; we would do well to ask ourselves what we can give up in order to help and enrich others by our own poverty. Let us not forget that real poverty hurts: no self-denial is real without this dimension of penance. I distrust a charity that costs nothing and does not hurt.[51]

Interesting. The Pope says we bear witness to the Gospel message of mercy "*to the extent that we imitate Christ who became poor and enriched us by his poverty.*" In other words, if we're truly going to live the mercy we've been reflecting on throughout this book, we need to give until it hurts. This does not mean we have to empty our bank accounts and give it all away. In fact, if we have a family to support, such action would be a sin. So, what does it mean?

As the Pope says, it means asking ourselves, "What can I give up in order to help and enrich others by my own poverty?" In other words, it means that *true almsgiving is related to fasting*. In true almsgiving, there's a direct correlation between what we give up and what we give. Both are important. It's like conversion. Conversion always involves turning away from something (sin) and turning toward someone else (God). It's not enough just to turn to God; we also have to turn away from sin. Conversely, it's not enough just to turn away from sin; we also have to turn to God. In a similar way, true almsgiving is not just about what we give but also about what we give up. If we're truly giving up, not from our surplus but from what costs us, then almsgiving becomes real for us. We feel it. And then, we receive the blessing.

Of course, what we give and give up doesn't just have to involve money. Our alms can also be our time and talents. For instance, we can give up an evening when we would normally watch TV and, instead, volunteer to teach religious education at the parish. The possibilities are endless. Unfortunately, endless possibilities don't help us come up with concrete action items, which is what this book is about (mercy in action). So, at this point, I'd like to begin to propose something concrete that every one of us can do and that's particularly relevant to our modern situation.

*P*ROJECT *R*ANSOM. When I was in college, I participated in an exciting, student-led initiative that eventually involved the majority of the campus, teachers and students alike. Called "Project Ransom," it took its inspiration from St. Pope John

Paul II's encyclical letter *The Gospel of Life*, and it changed the lives of countless students, even helping to inspire some, like myself, to pursue priestly and religious vocations.

Now, Project Ransom is not my proposal for us here. However, I'd like to share the general idea of this project, because some of its concepts and principles will relate to what I will propose for us to do in the next section, "Project Mercy." So let's get started.

I said Project Ransom took its inspiration from *The Gospel of Life*. The ideas of this letter are what really inspired and changed the lives of the students. In another book,[52] I shared my own testimony to the life-changing effect this letter had on me, which I'd like to re-present in the next several paragraphs, because it captures some of the key principles of the project.

The life-changing moment began as soon as I read the introduction to the letter, where John Paul describes its purpose. What struck me was not just what he said but how he said it. See for yourself:

> The present encyclical ... [is] meant to be a *precise and vigorous reaffirmation of the value of each human life and its inviolability*, and at the same time a pressing appeal addressed to each and every person, in the name of God: *respect, protect, love and serve life, every human life!* Only in this direction will you find justice, development, true freedom, peace and happiness!
>
> May these words reach all the sons and daughters of the Church! May they reach all people of good will who are concerned for the good of every man and woman and for the destiny of the whole of society! ...
>
> To all the members of the Church ... I make this most urgent appeal, that together we may offer this world of ours new signs of hope, and work to ensure that justice and solidarity will increase and that a new culture of human life will be affirmed,

for the building of an authentic civilization of truth and love.[53]

I can't adequately describe the impression these words made on me as a sophomore in college. Here was the Pope himself addressing an average guy like me with a "most urgent" and "pressing" appeal "in the name of God." Not only that, I didn't think Popes used so many exclamation points! And so I said to myself, "Man, this must be really important." I mean, as a practicing Catholic, I was pro-life and everything, but I didn't fully realize the situation was so serious. The Pope was talking in a much more forceful way than I ever would've expected, and as I read on, I continued to be blown away by his message.

In the subsequent chapters of the encyclical, John Paul described a historical drama of incredible proportions that's unfolding in our time. I was surprised to find him speaking in terms of a "profound crisis of culture,"[54] a "war,"[55] a "dramatic struggle,"[56] and even a "conspiracy."[57] He warned that modern man is living in a period in which "a long historical process is reaching a turning-point" with "tragic consequences."[58] Indeed, he explained that we ought to be "fully aware" that we are facing "an enormous and dramatic clash between good and evil, death and life, the 'culture of death' and the 'culture of life.'"[59]

At the time I read the Pope's words, I was not "fully aware" of any problem. In fact, I was really quite *unaware*. I mean, life seemed great. I had my friends, my classes, a chapel right on campus, and a fully-loaded cafeteria for my meals. Back home, my family was healthy and doing well. What more could I ask for? Yet John Paul II was talking about this "enormous and dramatic clash." What? Where? Not only that, he was saying that we are "all involved and we all share in it," and each person has the "inescapable responsibility" of choosing between the "culture of death" and the "culture of life." With Moses, he was exhorting me: "Choose life that you and your descendants may live" (Deut 30:19).[60] Yet he was also making it clear that simply choosing life isn't enough. Indeed, he was calling me to action, and his words left no doubt about what's at stake:

> [T]he challenge facing us is an arduous one: only the concerted efforts of all those who believe in the value of life can prevent a setback of unforeseeable consequences for civilization.[61]

This Pope was rocking my world. I'd never heard anything like this. He opened my eyes to the fact that I had to choose. I had to be involved. I had to act. But how? What was I supposed to do? What was I supposed to choose, concretely? How could I combat the culture of death and build a culture of life? One key passage from the encyclical answered these questions and provided the blueprint for Project Ransom:

> In a word, we can say that the cultural change which we are calling for demands from everyone the courage to *adopt a new lifestyle*, consisting in making practical choices … on the basis of a correct scale of values: *the primacy of being over having, of the person over things.* This renewed lifestyle involves a passing from *indifference to concern for others, from rejection to acceptance of them.* Other people are not rivals from whom we must defend ourselves, but brothers and sisters to be supported. They are to be loved for their own sakes, and they enrich us by their very presence.[62]

Here, then, is what Project Ransom was all about: *adopting a new lifestyle.* To me and my fellow students who had grown up in the culture of death, Project Ransom meant beginning to pull ourselves away from this culture. It meant saying no to the lifestyle of the culture of death with its focus on selfishness, consumerism, "having," and mere things. It meant saying yes to the lifestyle of the culture of life with its focus on self-giving, the person, and concern for those in need.

Naturally, this meant "making practical choices" for life, for love, and for others. Well, Project Ransom gave us something very concrete to do, together, to meet these goals. Here's how it worked.

Let's say you were a student on our campus, heard about Project Ransom, and wanted to join up. What would you do? Essentially, you would commit yourself to giving up at least one thing from our consumer culture for a year as a way of weaning yourself away from the culture. What thing? We recommended *soft drinks*. Why? Well, because the ads for soft drinks, such as those for Coca-Cola, were omnipresent. They were all over campus, on soda machines, and in the eating areas. They continuously played on the radio and TV. We'd see them on trucks and buses, in the stores, and along the street. They were everywhere, and once you decided to give up what they advertised, you'd notice them even more. And that was the point.

"Pro-life" Coke ad.

Since we didn't have much money, we figured we'd tap into the multi-million dollar advertising campaigns that were already out there but change their meaning by giving up their products. In other words, whenever we sacrificed a product (in most cases, again, it was soft drinks), the ads became a reminder to us of our commitment to life. We'd see the ad, "Always, Coca-Cola," and think, "Nope, always Jesus." We'd see the ad, "Pepsi, gotta have it!" and think, "Nope, gotta have a culture of life." Maybe that's a bit cheesy, but it worked. And it worked because we were no longer dealing with some vague idea about the culture of life or the culture of death. Rather, the battle between these cultures became something concrete, personal, and real to us, especially because of another aspect of the program: the unborn.

While the victims of the culture of death are vast and varied, Project Ransom focused its attention on unborn babies, because they are clearly the most innocent and defenseless victims of all. Let me explain this focus of the project a bit more.

For us college students studying at a solidly Catholic university, abortion was something we were all deeply saddened by, but it was also one of those things that was way too painful to dwell on. Of course, it broke our hearts, and what made matters worse is that it seemed there was nothing we could do about it. I mean, our unborn brothers and sisters were being killed by the *hundreds of millions worldwide*, and it seemed that we were powerless to do anything. And what do you do when you feel powerless to stop a tragedy? You look away. You try not to think about it. In fact, it can even be hard to pray about it, because it may seem like, "Well, what can my little prayers do?"

One of the main Scripture passages for our Project Ransom movement was an account from the Gospel of John, which indirectly addresses the idea, "Well, what can my little efforts do in the face of a Goliath like the culture of death?"

Lifting up his eyes, then, and seeing that a multitude was coming to him, Jesus said to Philip, "How

are we to buy bread, so that these people may eat?"
This he said to test him, for he himself knew what
he would do. Philip answered him, "Two hundred
denarii would not buy enough bread for each of
them to get a little." One of his disciples, Andrew,
Simon Peter's brother, said to him, "There is a
young boy here who has five barley loaves and two
fish; but what are they among so many?" Jesus said,
"Make the people sit down" (Jn 6:5-10).

We know the rest of the story. Jesus fed the multitude
with the small gift of a little boy. Well, for those of us who
were participating in Project Ransom, we believed that
while our little sacrifices were small, the Lord could make
them into something big for the kingdom. This was the
first and most important focus in Project Ransom: doing
something, even something small. We felt that while giving
up soft drinks might not be much, at least it was something.
And after doing *something*, we began to feel strengthened
and inspired to do more. In fact, seeing all the advertisements for the very thing we'd given up actually became a
powerful reminder to us of our sacrifice, of our commitment
to building a culture of life, and of our solidarity with the
unborn — and their mothers.

That was another important aspect of Project Ransom: a
fund for the mothers. We didn't just give up the soft drinks for
a year. Each of us also took the money we normally would have
spent on them for the year ($50-$100 per student) and donated
it to "the fund." The goal of the fund was to support women
in crisis pregnancies. Our thinking was that if we were truly
going to be pro-life, if we were actually going to encourage
women in crisis pregnancies to choose life, then we had to be in
solidarity with them, too. We couldn't just be sipping away on
a Coke, listening to our music in our designer clothes, and say
to them, "Hey, keep your baby!" when that often meant they
themselves would have to make a lot of sacrifices. Where was
the solidarity in that? So, at least to begin, we made a sacrifice

of something small and took the money we would have spent and offered it as financial support to those women.

So that's how it worked — and it was effective. To this day, I don't see soft drink advertisements in the same way, and they still remind me to pull myself away from the culture of death and support a culture of life. Also, I like to think that the several vocations that came out of Project Ransom were part of the miracles of grace the Lord worked with our little offerings. Perhaps you wouldn't be reading this book right now had I not said yes to giving up Coke for a year.

PROJECT MERCY. Like many idealistic initiatives started by young people, Project Ransom eventually fizzled out. The student leaders graduated, moved on to other things, and life went on. I think, though, that several of the principles of Project Ransom are still worth applying today. In fact, I propose that we apply them now as a work of mercy, a form of almsgiving that I call "Project Mercy." Before I explain how it works, though, let me first highlight some of the main points of Project Ransom that are especially important for works of mercy.

First, we need to realize that all of us, to one degree or another, are too caught up in our consumer culture. If we live in a developed country, we almost certainly will be tempted to choose having over being and mere things over the person. In fact, I think most of us could probably do well to trim some of the fat off our purchasing. Do we really need to buy another outfit when we have a closet full of clothes? Do we really need that bag of junk food? Do we really need to go out to see that new film with questionable morals? I'm not saying we reject all the creature comforts of life. No. Many recreational purchases can renew us and support the communion of family and friends. It's just that there are probably some ways that we overdo it, especially in view of our present cultural context.

The culture of death is still with us. In fact, it's even stronger than when I was in college. And because of the wide-spread influence of its doctrine of selfishness, people are even more lonely, broken, and hurting today. In view of this reality, we should especially view our purchasing against the backdrop of the needs of others. Yes, there's that new album on iTunes, but is there someone I could help with that money instead? "Oh," we say, "but I can get the album *and* help that person. I have enough money." Okay, but then we're giving from our surplus and not from our poverty. Then the gift doesn't hurt — yet, as we've learned, it's better if it hurts us a bit.

"Oh," we say, "well, that iTunes album is right here, glowing on my computer screen, but I don't see any poor people. If I see them, then I'll help them." That may be the case, but we need to be proactive in our works of mercy. We can't just wait for people to come to us. Believe me, the ads for products will certainly come to us. But the needs of the hungry, the stranger, the naked, the sick, and the imprisoned do not have flashy ads that pop up on our computer and TV screens.

Alright, so what do we do? Well, that's where Project Mercy comes in. And here's how it works: *Read this book.* That's it! In a sense, this book *is* Project Mercy, but you won't fully understand what I mean until you read the conclusion that follows. In the conclusion, "Hunt, Gather, Go!" you're going to put together a mercy action plan, part of which will involve what I call "The Mercy Fund." That fund is basically a piggy bank at home or an account at your bank where you put all the proceeds from your sacrifices that will fund your works of mercy. What works of mercy? The ones you've already been checking off in the "Action Items" sections of this book!

Your Mercy Fund.

Okay, so here's how you build your Mercy Fund. Let's say you choose to sacrifice soft drinks, donuts, or gourmet coffee for six months. Well, then you'll put the money you would have spent on those things into your Mercy Fund. Let's say you give up going to see a movie and decide to make a Holy Hour instead. Well, then you put the money you would have spent on the movie into your Mercy Fund. Let's say you get the cheapo shampoo instead of the high-end stuff. Make a note of it, and then put the savings into your Mercy Fund. That's how it works: funds from sacrifices, alms that actually cost you something, cash from foregoing luxuries — and all of it goes to works of mercy!

I'll say more about the Mercy Fund in the conclusion, but for now, I'd like to conclude this chapter by addressing two pressing questions: (1) *"How much should I give?"* and (2) *"To whom should I give?"* The first question is pretty easy to answer. The general rule-of-thumb, based on Sacred Scripture, is that we should "tithe." In other words, it's suggested that we give 10 percent of our earnings to charity. More specifically, I've heard that half of the 10 percent should go to one's parish and the other half to support various works of mercy. (Of course, we're always free to give more — 10 percent is just the suggested minimum.)

The second question, "To whom should I give?" is not so easy to answer. After all, there are millions of worthy organizations, projects, and people who would love to have our support. Amid so many options, *how does one choose?*

*F*IVE PRINCIPLES FOR GIVING. Let me start off by saying that I actually can't give an answer to this question. Where you give your time, treasure, and talents is ultimately something between you and the Lord. What I *can* do is offer some principles, in no particular order, that may be helpful to you in your discernment.

(1) Keep It Close to Home — the Principle of Subsidiarity. No, I'm not discouraging you from giving to the needy in other countries or in other parts of our own country. In fact, the greatest need may be far away. (See the third principle.) Still, there is something to supporting those who are closest to you.

A fundamental principle of the Church's social teaching is called "the principle of subsidiarity," which basically means that problems in human society should be handled at the lowest possible level, closest to those who are affected. For instance, the federal government shouldn't get involved with problems that the states can handle; states shouldn't get involved with problems that cities can handle; cities shouldn't get involved with problems that families can handle.

So, inspired by the principle of subsidiarity, one might ask, "What are the problems that I'm closest to and can handle?" For instance, maybe the needs of a family member, next door neighbor, or coworker come to mind. Well, that's a start. Maybe that's where you should give. But as you think about it, also keep in mind that in some cases you don't really need to think about it. It's a no-brainer. Why? Because there are probably some people you are *obligated* to help. For instance, a parent ought to provide for the needs (not necessarily the wants) of his or her own family before giving to others in need. Also, in most cases, a parishioner should contribute to his own parish even before contributing to other organizations. Having said that, these kinds of obligations do not give us the green light to be stingy with those in need. ("I give to my family" is no excuse to ignore the poor.)

(2) Give to Those Who Have Given to You — the Principle of Gratitude. All of us have benefited from the merciful deeds of others, and it's certainly a good thing to show our gratitude. So, I recommend asking yourself, "What works-of-mercy organizations have helped me?" For instance, maybe you attended a Catholic university that nourished your faith, clothed your ignorance, and trained you for a successful profession. It's good to give back (provided the university hasn't apostasized,

as many have done). Maybe you experienced a conversion
through a Catholic television network. It's good to give back.
Maybe you were deeply inspired by the work of a certain congregation of religious sisters. Again, it's good to give back.

*(3) Give to Those in Greatest Need — the Preferential
Option for the Poor.* Inspired by the merciful love of the Heart
of Jesus, the Church calls us to a "preferential love" for those
who are poor and in greatest need. These "least ones" should
always be on our hearts and minds if not because of our overflowing love for them, then at least because we know that we
will be judged based on our treatment of them. (See, again, Mt
25:31-46.)

So who are they? Where are the greatest needs? These are
important questions to bring before the Lord. After all, how
one uses his financial means is serious business. Indeed, the
Lord will demand from each one of us an accounting of how
we used our resources. He will want to know whether we gave
thoughtlessly or conscientiously, with the greatest good and
greatest needs in mind. (By the way, it's interesting to note that
in the Gospel of Matthew, the parable of the talents, which calls
us to be responsible with our resources, immediately precedes
the Last Judgment scene that begins this book.)

(4) Give Yourself — Almsgiving in Action. It's one thing
to give a check to an organization that does a work of mercy.
It's quite another to give oneself. Whenever people used to ask
Blessed Mother Teresa of Calcutta how they could help the
poor, she'd always answer, "Make it cash." No. Of course, she
didn't say that. Rather, she'd say, "Come and see." In other
words, she wanted people to be actively involved in the works
of mercy.

So, if you can give not just your treasure but your time
and talents as well, then do it. Truly, to combine your support
of a worthy organization with your own personal involvement
is a "win-win." For example, if there's a pamphlet about the
faith that really touches your heart, buy a hundred of them

(support) and give them away to others (personal involvement). And if you want a win-win-win, then use the money
to buy those pamphlets from the sacrificial offerings of your
Mercy Fund, instead of just drawing from your surplus.

*(5) Give the Lord a Chance to Speak — the Principle of
Prayer.* Once you've carefully considered all these principles for
giving, ask the Holy Spirit for wisdom in discerning his will for
how you can best give your time, treasure, and talents to those
who are most in need. Don't rush it, but take a good amount
of time to bring this area of your life before the Lord and really
seek his direction. Consider all your options and resources as
you apply the principles for giving. The conclusion that follows
will assist you as you begin this process.

As we close this section, it may be helpful to call to
mind the parable of the talents from Matthew's Gospel (see
25:14-30), especially the Lord's words to those who used their
resources responsibly, "Well done, good and faithful servant;
you have been faithful over a little, I will set you over much;
enter into the joy of your master."

*A*ND *S*PEAKING OF *A*LMSGIVING...

> *You may find the Marians' website **GiftofMercy.org**
> helpful. This website lists ways you can support the
> works of mercy of my community, the Marian Fathers
> of the Immaculate Conception.*

*C*ONTINUE THE *S*TORY...

> *To learn more about Project Ransom, Project Mercy,
> and more, visit **MercyPages.org** and click "Continue
> the Story."*

~ Action Items ~
Almsgiving
[Check the box next to any of the action items below
that you might actually be able to do.]

☐ I will get a Mercy Fund bank and put it in my house. I will
use a…

    ☐ Piggy bank

    ☐ Cookie jar

    ☐ Vase

    ☐ Other: _____

☐ I will give up some food or drink as a sacrifice.

    → What food or drink? _____

    → For how long? _____

    → At what value? $ _____
    [Reminder: Don't forget to put this money into your Mercy
    Fund.]

☐ I will give up eating out.

    → For how long? Or how many times? _____

    → At what value? $ _____

☐ I will give up some luxury cosmetic, perfume, or clothing
item.

    → Which one(s)? _____

    → For how long? _____

    → At what value? $ _____

☐ I will give up some form of entertainment.

    ☐ Movies

       → For how long? _____

       → At what value? $ _____

☐ Cable subscription (or downgrade)

→ For how long? _____

→ At what value? $ _____

☐ Magazine subscription

→ For how long? _____

→ At what value? $ _____

☐ Other

→ For how long? _____

→ At what value? $ _____

☐ I will start using coupons and deposit the money I save into my Mercy Fund.

☐ I will have a garage sale for things I don't need and will transfer the proceeds to my Mercy Fund.

☐ I will keep track of other sacrifices as they come up and put the proceeds into my Mercy Fund.

☐ Other ideas: _____

_____

_____

_____

_____

_____

PART THREE

Conclusion

Hunt, Gather, Go!

*L*EFT, *R*IGHT, OR *C*AUGHT IN THE *M*IDDLE? Let's begin this conclusion by reading the very first verses of the Scripture passage we saw at the outset of this book:

> When the Son of man comes in his glory, and all the angels with him, then he will sit on his glorious throne. Before him will be gathered all the nations, and he will separate them one from another as a shepherd separates the sheep from the goats, and he will place the sheep at his right hand, but the goats at the left. Then the king will say…

What will he say? The blessing and the curse. He will give the blessing of eternal life to those on his right who fed him, gave him drink, welcomed him, clothed him, cared for him, and visited him. He will punish with the curse of eternal fire those on his left who did not feed him, did not give him drink, did not welcome him, did not clothe him, did not care for him, and did not visit him.

And where will we be? On the left? On the right? Maybe *caught in the middle*? What do I mean by "caught in the middle"? Well, perhaps we've come to this point in the book, filled in the boxes of the action items, and then… and then that's the last we ever look at them. I think we've all done something like that. We've made our New Year's resolutions, even written them out, and then… nothing. Or, filled with zeal, we've ended a retreat, had a list of resolutions, and then… we do nothing. We forget all about them.

That can't happen this time. Why not? Because then we really might end up caught in the middle.

On the last day, when the Lord separates the sheep from the goats, he may come across some who, seeing themselves herded toward the goats, will cry out, "Lord, Lord! Lord, it's me! Don't you know me? I'm with the sheep! I mean, I had all these *plans* to help you. I even read a book about doing works of mercy, and I had some great action items. My *intentions* were good!" To these, Jesus speaks sobering words,

"Not everyone who says to me, 'Lord, Lord,' shall enter the kingdom of heaven, but he who does the will of my Father who is in heaven" (Mt 7:21).

So, by "caught in the middle," I'm referring to those who will be "caught" in their lack of resolve, lack of follow through in doing what is right. There's a saying that "the way to hell is paved with good intentions." Truly, we can have great plans and good intentions, but if we don't actually DO them, then that's a problem. It's the difference between being "hearers" and "doers" of the word. (See Mt 7:24-27; Jas 1:22.) And if we just listen to it, what good is that? Being caught in the middle is as good as being separated and put on the left, with the goats.

This conclusion is about helping us not to get caught in the middle but to be *doers* of what we've learned. In fact, the action starts now with three activities: *hunting, gathering,* and then the *doing* itself. Before we begin, though, let's start with a fourth activity that's most important of all: praying. Let us pray…

> Heavenly Father, I thank you and praise you for the gift of my life and the gift of new life in Jesus Christ, your Son and my Savior. Out of gratitude and love, I want to serve you and do your will in my life.
>
> You know, Lord, that apart from you, I can do nothing. Aware of my weakness, I beg for the grace to fulfill your will in my life. I beg for the gift of the Holy Spirit to enlighten my mind, so I may know the specific works of mercy you are calling me to do. I ask you to strengthen my will, so I will put them into action. I ask you to bless my heart, that every work of mercy I do will flow not from self-seeking and reward but out of a genuine love for you and for my neighbor.
>
> I ask all this in the name of Jesus Christ and through the intercession of Mary, my mother, as I pray: Hail Mary, full of grace…

*H*ᴜɴᴛ. Let's go hunting. Specifically, let's go back in this book and hunt for checked boxes. When you find one of these boxes, you're going to shoot it. Your weapon is your pen or pencil, and your ammo is as follows:

Wait, I thought we were hunting boxes, not pigs. Right! The "PIG$" are your ammo. Here's what I mean: Each one of the words and symbols above represents a category to mark off next to the checked boxes of your action items. Here's what each word or symbol stands for:

P = Prayer
I = Investigate
G = General
**$** = Purcha$e
⊕ = FIRE!

Now, more specifically, here's how the hunt happens. Go back in the book to all the "Action Items" sections. Then, hunt down the boxes you've marked off. When you come across one of them, read it, and then shoot it with one of the letters or symbols above. By "shoot," I mean write the appropriate letter or symbol in the margin right next to the box. And what's the appropriate letter or symbol? Well, if the action item involves a prayer action, then write "P" in the margin next to it. If it involves something that will need more investigation, such as research on the Internet, a phone call, or an e-mail, then write "I." If it involves just something to keep in mind, write "G." If it involves a purchase of some sort, write "$." If it's something that you can put on a list of action items now without having to do any research or investigation, then write an "X" with a circle around it. For example, your pages may look something like this:

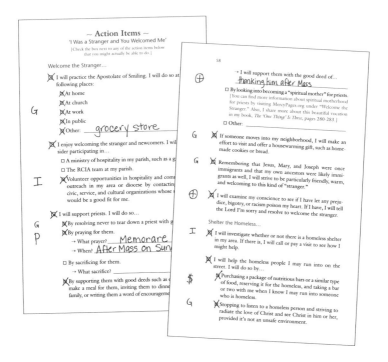

So, there you go. Now take your weapon in hand (pen or pencil), start turning those pages, and happy hunting!

Actually, before you go, here's a handy little map to help you locate the Action Items pages where your checked boxes are hiding:

I was hungry...
(pages 39-40)

I was sick...
(pages 81-82)

I was a stranger...
(pages 57-60)

I was in prison...
(pages 112-115)

I was naked...
(pages 70-74)

Almsgiving
(pages 132-133)

*G*ATHER. Once you're done hunting, you're going to want to gather up what you've shot and put it in its proper place. Here's what I mean. On the lined pages that follow this conclusion (the "Go! Pages"), you're going to write at the top of the first page "PRAYERS," and then, below that, you'll write down the prayer action items that you've marked with a "P" earlier in the book. (They don't have to be complete sentences, just enough so you understand and remember what they mean.)

When that is done, then you'll start the next section by simply writing "INVESTIGATE" at the end of the preceding section. Then, you'll write the investigation action items (the ones you marked "I") below the "INVESTIGATE" heading.

When that is done, you will NOT write a category for the "G's." Rather, you'll just go back in the book and either highlight them or circle them, so they'll stand out. These aren't really action items but just things for you to keep in mind. Highlighting or circling them will make them stand out as you go through this book in the future. (Yes, I do recommend reviewing these pages in the future.) Then, you continue with "PURCHA$E" and "FIRE" in the usual way on the lined sheets.

By the way, don't forget to use your Mercy Fund for funding your "purchase" action items. That way, the sacrifices you make will be going toward those in need, and you'll be combining almsgiving with real sacrifice. To this end, you might want to keep a space in the section under "PURCHA$E" for writing down the total amount of funds in your Mercy Fund, so you'll know how much money you have to spend on works of mercy.

My last recommendation is to look over the list *under each category* and rank the items according to their importance. You can do this by writing a "1" next to the action item that you think is most important, a "2" next to the one that is second in importance, and so on. This will help fend off the feeling that your action items are overwhelming. Please do not fall for this temptation! You do not need to accomplish everything you've written down, at least not immediately. The next section is going to explain what to do so you're not overwhelmed. (By the way, if it's not realistic for you to accomplish all your action items, you're certainly free to change your mind and cross some of them off your list.)

*G*o! Once you've hunted down your boxes, shot them all up, and gathered them into their appropriate places, then you're ready to get *go-ing*. You're ready to put mercy into action! But wait, how, specifically, do we implement our action items? Here's a seven-point list for you to follow:

- First, after you've filled up your Go! Pages, read through them one time without stopping, so you have a sense of the big picture of what's on your plate.

- Second, under each category of your Go! Pages, circle or highlight the ONE action item (or maybe two) that you can reasonably do first.

- Third, write down on a separate sheet of paper the main action item(s) you circled for each category. Let's call this your "Action Plan."

- Fourth, on your Action Plan, next to each action item, write down when, where, and how you are going to implement it. In other words, jot down your strategy. For example, let's say you're going to purchase an audio CD of Fr. Donald Calloway's conversion story to give to your nephew who is struggling with his faith. You would write down the website you need to visit (LighthouseCatholicMedia.org), when you'll visit it, when you'll give the CD to you nephew, how you'll give it to him, and so on. (I think you get the point that I'm highly recommending being very concrete with the implementation strategy of your Action Plan.)

- Fifth, after you have accomplished an action item on your Action Plan, then cross it off from both your Action Plan and your Go! Pages.

- Sixth, go back to your Go! Pages, find another item to add to your Action Plan, and repeat this process every time you accomplish one until all the items on your Go! Pages are crossed off.

- Seventh, read this book again, and refill your Go! Pages. (You'll probably need some blank sheets of paper.) As you refill them, be creative, and try to come up with action items that aren't listed in this book.

So there you go! Have fun going through your Go! Pages, and don't forget to periodically look back on your "Action Items" sections to keep the "G"s fresh in your mind. And speaking of action items, I have one last suggestion before we conclude.

Every night before going to bed, look at one of your hands and remember Blessed Mother Teresa's "five-finger Gospel," which is this:

More specifically, at the end of the day, as you look at your hand and remember these words, ask yourself whether or not you've reached out to perform at least one work of mercy. If you have, thank God. If not, tell the Lord you're sorry for this sin of omission, resolve to do better the next day, and conclude with a work of mercy that's always within your grasp: prayer. Pray for someone who is suffering, and ask the Lord to console that person with his grace.

Speaking of prayer, I'd like to close with a blessing for you and for all who will read this book:

> May the Lord bless you. May you receive his joy, and may your joy be full, the joy that flows from putting mercy into action. And may the Lord call each one of you on the last day:
>
> > "Come, O blessed of my Father, inherit the kingdom prepared for you from the foundation of the world; for I was hungry and you gave me food, I was thirsty and you gave me drink, I was a stranger and you welcomed me, I was naked and you clothed me, I was sick and you visited me, I was in prison and you came to me."
>
> In short, may you hear the Lord lovingly say,

"You did it to me."

GO! PAGES

Two points: (1) After completing your lists, again, don't feel overwhelmed. Simply follow the seven-point plan for implementing your action items on pages 142-143. (2) If you need more writing space than what is provided below, simply continue your Go! Pages on additional blank sheets of paper.

_____

_____

_____

_____

_____

_____

_____

_____

_____

_____

_____

_____

_____

_____

_____

_____

_____

_____

_____

_____

_____

_____

_____

_____

Out of space? Don't worry!
Simply get some blank sheets of paper and place them here.

APPENDIX ONE

The Three Degrees of
Mercy Explained

Jesus taught St. Faustina that there are three degrees of mercy: deed, word, and prayer. (See *Diary*, 742.) The following is an explanation of those three degrees, adapted from pages 143-159 of the book *Consoling the Heart of Jesus.*

1. Mercy in Deed: The Merciful Outlook

There are infinite ways of doing deeds of mercy. To give some organization to them, theologians have divided the "works of mercy" into two categories: spiritual and corporal. Each category, they say, contains seven works of mercy, making for a grand total of 14. (See page 26.) Yet reflecting on 14 points can be a lot of work. So, instead of fourteen points, I'd like to present just one simple and effective way of practicing deeds of mercy. I call it the "merciful outlook." I like this way a lot because it's a deed of mercy we can practice almost anytime (provided we're around other people). I also like it because it seems to fit so well with the Lord's strategy, which I'll now explain.

Many people today avoid the Lord, thinking that he must not love them because of their sins. They think God has rejected them, and so they've given up on trying to please him. Yet, even if they've given up on Jesus, he hasn't given up on them. If they're too afraid to go to him, he's decided to go to them. But in going to them, he's cautious because he knows that at even the slightest sign of him, they'll bolt. So Jesus goes to them incognito. Can you guess what disguise he uses? That's right, you and me. Jesus wants to love them through the way we look at them, through our merciful outlook. They probably won't immediately recognize that it's Jesus behind such a look (if they did, they'd bolt), but it can still have its healing effect, and it prepares their hearts to eventually recognize his loving face. Thus, the merciful outlook truly is part of the Lord's patient and loving strategy.

Now that we know something about the Lord's strategy, it should make even more sense why Jesus loves to heal our hearts, making them more compassionate. For, not only does such healing make us love him more, not only do we become much happier, but having a renewed heart helps us to develop a merciful outlook toward others. It helps us to look at others, especially at God's prodigal children, with Jesus' own love and compassion. Therefore, it truly is a way that we can console Jesus in the members of his Body. But developing the merciful outlook isn't easy. If we want to be good missionaries of the Lord's love and mercy, we need to come to a better understanding of what it is. Let's begin by considering what it's not.

The merciful outlook is not the "patronizing outlook." It's not about pitying people. Yes, mercy is love when it encounters suffering, but the merciful outlook is not about feeling sorry for people, and it's certainly not about looking down on them from some high pedestal of self-righteousness. As St. Pope John Paul II wrote in his encyclical letter *Dives in Misericordia*, true mercy is always a bilateral reality, a two-way street: As we give it, we also receive it. If we don't habitually realize this as we do deeds of mercy, then we just might be stuck in the patronizing outlook. To get unstuck (and thus to be free to live the merciful outlook), I recommend we spend some time pondering the Pope's actual words on bilateral mercy:

> We must also continually purify all our actions and all our intentions in which mercy is understood and practiced in a unilateral way, as a good done to others. An act of merciful love is only really such when we are deeply convinced at the moment that we perform it that we are at the same time receiving mercy from the people who are accepting it from us. If this bilateral and reciprocal quality is absent, our actions are not yet true acts of mercy, nor has there yet been fully completed in us that conversion to which Christ has shown us the way by His words and example, even to the Cross, nor are we yet sharing fully in the magnificent source of merciful love that has been revealed to us by Him.[63]

The merciful outlook is not the "over-spiritualized out-look." Sometimes people speak of loving Christ in others in a way that makes me a bit uncomfortable. Here's why. Imagine your spouse or a close friend seems especially kind and loving toward you, so you ask them, "Why do you love me so much?" And they reply, "Oh, I was loving Jesus *in* you." That sounds awfully close to, "I wasn't loving you. I was loving Jesus." Which might as well be, "You're chopped liver, but Jesus is lovable even in dead meat." If that's what's meant, then some-thing is surely missing.

The merciful outlook is not the "proselytizing outlook." For example, the approach of those who wear a salesman's smile and a slick badge that says "Elder Smith" is exactly what I do not mean by the merciful outlook. I'm not talking about phony friendliness that sees others through the agenda of winning converts. No, the merciful outlook, as we'll see, has to do with evangelization — not proselytizing. It has to do with proclaiming the good news of Christ's love through an authentic love for the other as a person. We'll get to that in due time. For now, having learned something of what the merciful outlook is not, let's explore what it is.

The outlook I'm describing is merciful because it responds to suffering. In fact, it's a compassionate response to what's probably the most universal and deepest human suffering, namely, existential loneliness. This needs some more explaining.

I think the best way to describe man's existential loneli-ness (and man in general) is with one simple word: thirst. Man is a "thirst," and his thirst, unlike that of animals, is not fully quenched by the things of this world. For example, let's say we give Fido the dog a nice yard, food, water, and lots of affection. Of course, his tail will just keep on wagging. It's not so with us. We can have everything and still be depressed, still be thirsting for what we can't quite put into words.

Saint Augustine, brilliant writer that he was, could put the problem into words. In one of the most famous lines in Chris-tian literature, he wrote, "You made us for Yourself, O Lord, and our hearts are restless until they rest in You."[64] We all have restless hearts, a seemingly unquenchable thirst, because we're made for God. We're made to be with him in heaven. We're made to see him face-to-face. Right now, however, we're not there. We're not fully with him, and we can't fully see him. So, in this land of exile, we experience a deep and sometimes agonizing existential loneliness.

Like St. Augustine, the French philosopher Blaise Pascal had an amazing way with words. Also like Augustine, he explained man's existential loneliness with astonishing clarity. Writing in the 17th century at a time when kings held absolute power in their dominions and everyone seemed to envy them, Pascal came up with an insightful theory to explain why everyone wants to be king.[65] He said everyone wants to be king because kings can wage wars, conduct the affairs of state, throw big parties, and always be surrounded by a whirlwind of people. In other words, the king gets to be perpetually distracted. Distracted from what? Distracted from the fact of his unhappiness, his existential loneliness.

Pascal held that the worst torture for modern man is to be quiet and alone in his own room.[66] Why? Because solitude brings out the beast of our loneliness. Of course, even in the midst of distraction, the beast is still there gnawing at our hearts. (Even in the middle of a crowd, we can often feel him chewing away.) But distraction helps numb us to his constant gnawing. Thus, people in Pascal's day envied the king, and in our day, people still want to live like kings. Yes, with our cell phones, iPods, and e-mail, some might say we've become "royally good" at distracting ourselves.

Christ teaches another way. He tells us we don't have to numb the pain of our loneliness. He calls out to us, "I can quench your thirst! I can give your hearts rest!" (see Jn 7:47; Mt 11:28). He can say this in full truth because he's God, the one for whom we're made, the one for whom we thirst. Specifically, he's Jesus Christ, God the Son become flesh, and he's been sent by God the Father through the power of God the Holy Spirit to bring us into their Family of Love, the Holy Trinity.

Jesus says to us: "I did not create you to be alone. I created you for communion in my Family of Love." Such words are not pie in the sky, not a future fulfillment we only get when we die. No. Christ comes now in Word and Sacrament — especially in the Sacrament of Holy Communion — to give us the joy the world cannot give. Christ also comes now through you and through me, through communion with friends and family, thus giving us a real (though limited) satisfaction to our longing, quench to our thirst, and rest to our hearts. It's precisely here that the merciful outlook comes in as a response to people's loneliness.

The merciful outlook is a way of giving drink to the thirsty. It gives a cup of love to another and to ourselves as we make our pilgrimage through this desert of life to the Ocean of Love, the Holy Trinity. I said it provides a cup. The merciful outlook is not a gushing bucket of smother love. It's a cup. It's a simple thing but beautiful to a thirsty heart. It's a subtle way of seeing others — not an intense staring — that communicates to them a simple and sincere message, "I delight that you exist." This modest expression of real delight in the very existence of the other will often be for them a refreshing cup of love, a cup that helps to quench their thirst and point them along the way to the Eternal Fountain of delight-filled Love that alone truly satisfies.

Now, some people may be getting troubled at this point. They may be honing in on how the merciful outlook is a way of seeing others with delight, which may cause them to think, "Wait a minute, delight is a feeling." (People often get nervous about feelings.) In fact, they may be saying to themselves: "He's not suggesting we're always supposed to be feeling delight in others, is he? After all, what matters is not what we feel anyway, right? What truly matters is simply that we choose to love, that we will it." In response to such thoughts, I'd say, "Yes, it's true that sometimes love must be expressed without feeling. Sometimes it's simply a dry but firm decision of the will." (Thus, we've all probably heard the expression, "Love is a choice.") However, I'd also say that love simply as a choice is not the ideal. Ideally, love ought to be felt.

Think about it. Unless we ourselves feel love for the other, will our love still carry the warmth that touches hearts? I don't think so. People are good at distinguishing felt love from forced love. The merciful outlook just doesn't work without true feeling — and it can't be faked. Phony smiles that say "You're just so special!" (gag) do not work. Thus, an important question arises, "How do we feel delight in others?" This question brings us to the essence of the merciful outlook.

Felt delight in others, expressed in the merciful outlook, stems from grasping the truth and beauty of the authentic self of the other. And who is the other? The other is Christ. Yet I don't mean the other is Christ in an over-spiritualized kind of way. (There's no ghost-like Christ hiding behind the other's ear.) No, the other is Christ. Christ is not hiding. The other is Christ insofar as he's a member of Christ's Mystical Body (or, if he's not a Christian, he's a prospective member of Christ by virtue of his being made in the image of God and called to full membership in Christ's Body). Of course, the other is not the same as Christ the *Head* of the Body. Still, to be a member of Christ's Body is truly to be Christ. Regarding this point, it's helpful to reflect once again on Christ's startling words to Saul (later St. Paul) who had been persecuting Christians, "Saul, Saul, why are you persecuting me?" (Acts 9:4). The Lord didn't say, "Hey, Saul, why are you persecuting my followers?" Rather, he said, "Why are you persecuting *me*?"

So, the member of Christ's Body is Christ. The word "is" here is important. The merciful outlook I'm proposing takes it seriously. For this outlook aims to discover the other person as a unique member of the Body of Christ. As a member (or potential member) of Christ's Body, the other person shows forth an utterly unique facet of the mystery of Christ. I'll now say more about this, for this is precisely that in which we should feel our delight when we delight in another person. It's also what helps turn the over-spiritualized outlook into the merciful outlook.

A Christian ought to delight in Christ. He ought to have drunk deeply of the beauty, goodness, and glory of Christ

Jesus. He ought always to be eager to have more of Christ, that is, to know him more fully so as to love him more deeply. Well, the members of the Body of Christ help us to know and love Christ more. I say that because each and every human being is created in the image of God and given a vocation to manifest by his redeemed existence a facet of the beauty of Christ in a way that no other being in the cosmos is capable of doing. What an amazing vocation each person has! No wonder Christ longs for us to become saints, for a saint is someone who most perfectly fulfills this vocation. A saint manifests the unique face of Christ he or she is called to be. Thus, a saint helps reveal Christ to us, and Christ is so beautiful in his saints.

"But wait just a minute," someone might say, "Isn't Christ enough? Why do I need other people to show me Christ?" Yes, Christ is enough. That is, the full Christ is enough, Christ head and members (see Eph 4:13). For Christ and the members of his Body truly are one (see 1 Cor 12:12-27), and to know and love Christ is not only to know and love Christ the Head but also to know and love his members. Those other people are him. They're his Body. Clearly, we don't express true love for someone by saying, "From the neck up, I'm in love with you. As for the rest, well, all I feel is hate." Similarly, we don't love Christ if we say, "I love Christ the Head of the Mystical Body but despise the members of his body." Saint John calls such a person "a liar" (1 Jn 4:20). Love, then, is of the whole body, head and members. We can't truly love the one without also loving the others.

Now, let's address from a different angle the question, "Why do I need other people to show me Christ?" Look at it this way: Christ is like the sun. His brightness, like the sun's, is so great that we may only be able to gaze on his full glory for a short while. Yet, just as we can easily take in the sun's marvelous light as it bathes the beauties of creation and thus have a better appreciation and gratitude for the gift of the sun, so also we can easily see the marvelous beauty of Christ in his saints and thus have a better appreciation, knowledge, and love of Christ. In the Christian dispensation, more is not less. Rather, more is more! And the beauty of Christ in his members gives us limited beings even more ways to take in and contemplate his infinite richness.

Still, it's true that God didn't have to make things this way. Christ didn't have to invite us to such close intimacy with himself that we become his very Body. God could have forgiven our sins but then left us as mere creatures and slaves — thank God that's not what he did. Thank God that God in Christ Jesus no longer calls us creatures but "children of God" (1 Jn 3:1), no longer calls us slaves but "friends" (Jn 15:15). Thank God he not only forgives our sins but raises us up to his own divine life and makes us members of his Body. This, thanks be to the unfathomable mercy of God, is now the way things are. No, it didn't have to be this way. God didn't have to do it like this, but it's how he did do it. By God's good pleasure and design, it is reality. Christ is now glorious not only in himself but in his members, and this doesn't take anything away from him. In fact, it helps us to appreciate him all the more not only for the super-abundant mercy that created this new situation but for the amazing richness of Christ that this situation reveals.

"Okay, fine," someone may say, "I can accept that the saints reveal Christ's glory. Yes, Christ is beautiful in his saints ... but not in everyday people." Not true. The glory of God and the beauty of Christ fill all creation. It's just more of a challenge to see this glory in those people who don't manifest it as overwhelmingly as do the saints. This is the challenge of living the merciful outlook. It takes practice. It takes grace. It takes begging for the gift of grace.

We really can have the merciful outlook. The saints had it, and we're called to be saints. We're called to see as they see. And how did they see? They saw as God sees. And how does God see? He sees the beauty of what he created (see Gen 1:31). In an unrepentant sinner, he still sees a vocation to greatness even if it's tragically entombed in a hardened heart. Amazingly, when such a sinner recognizes that God sees this greatness in him, he begins to come alive. Such is the gaze of God. Such is the power of mercy. Such is the meaning and power of the merciful outlook. It draws out the good and brings back to life. It's a God-like gazing on others that draws out their goodness and brings them into the new and more abundant life.

Sometimes this God-like gaze is terrible. It's terrible not in the sense of "that movie was terrible" but in the weighty sense of that "terrible day" when Christ comes again on the clouds of heaven with trumpet blasts (see Mt 24:30-31). For the merciful outlook does indeed bring with it a kind of reckoning. It's not yet the "terrible day of reckoning" — thank God — but it's like it. For the person who receives the merciful outlook from another sees reflected in the eyes of the other the words, "You are great."[67] However, these words are also a call to greatness. For, while the greatness is truly there — the other person sees it! — it's not fully there.

The person who receives the merciful outlook knows that the greatness he sees reflected back at him in the eye of the other is tragically not all there in him, because he can also feel the gaze of his own "inner eye," his conscience. This inner eye makes him tragically aware of not being who he's meant to be, which is terrible. Yet it's not despairingly terrible. For there's still the gaze of the other, at least in memory, constantly echoing the words, "You are great." So the person feels himself in the midst of the terrible drama of having to choose either to be the person he presently is or the person he's called to become, either the person of mediocrity or the awe-inspiring person he was destined to be from before the foundation of the world (see Mt 25:34; Eph 1:4).

The terrible aspect of the merciful outlook leads us to an important point: It's not our job to see in the other what the other's own inner eye sees. In fact, we can't do it. Our gaze can't penetrate to the inner sanctuary of another's conscience, and we ought not to try. For not only are we incapable of doing it, but there's a penalty if we try. Another's conscience is sacred space the Lord himself guards. If we try to enter it — for instance, with our rash judgments — we pay a heavy price. We pay the price of losing some, if not all, of our ability to exercise the merciful outlook, and our own hearts harden.

Sadly, the other person also pays a price when we presume to know how his conscience convicts him. For just as the merciful outlook can give life and draw out the good, the judgmental outlook can draw darkness out of the other and even destroy him. It can crushingly magnify his inner eye's verdict of guilt. It can help tempt him to believe that who he is at his core is really the evil the judgmental outlook thinks it's discovered there, and thus it can extinguish hope. In fact, seeing the other's look of disdain, the person living under the harsh stare of the judgmental outlook will often say to himself, "Well, I guess that's just who I am." And then he'll stop striving for the greatness that's his call.

When we look at others with the judgmental outlook, we abandon our part in the Lord's patient and loving strategy, which I mentioned earlier. We go, instead, to assist in someone else's strategy, a sinister, destructive strategy. Although we don't want to do this, how can we avoid it? For surely there are signs in others of what's inconsistent with their vocation in Christ — and at least we can point to things about them that annoy us.

Can people be annoying? Yes. Do people sin? Yes. As for the annoying stuff, we need to deal with it, look past it, or maybe even rediscover it as treasure. As for the sinful stuff, we leave that up to the Lord and them — unless, of course, we have a clear responsibility to confront or correct them, in which case we need to beg the Holy Spirit for grace and prudence and then do our duty lovingly. Most of the time, however, I think our responsibility lies in deep-sea diving.

In overcoming temptations to go from the merciful to the judgmental outlook, it's good to be like a deep-sea diver who searches for sunken treasure. Such a diver knows there's treasure down there, and he goes for it. Sometimes he has to swim through dark, murky water and even fend off underwater beasts, but he keeps going. He knows the treasure's worth.

As we've already learned, in each person there's an invaluable treasure, a facet of the face of Christ that can't be found in anyone else. In the saints, no diving is necessary to find it — at some point a volcano of love erupted in them and pushed its way up to the surface, becoming a beautiful tropical island that displays its abundant treasure right there on the sun-swept beach. In most of us, however, the treasure is still underwater, and it may even be lying on the ocean floor. But it's down there, and it's worth diving for. We need not fear the murky water (the hardness of the other's heart) nor pay attention to the sea monsters (the other's annoying personality traits). If the sharks come out (meanness or signs of certain kinds of inappropriateness), we don't have to stay (and sometimes we shouldn't), but the little bites from the other sea monsters are nothing compared to the delight that comes from finding the treasure that lies on the ocean floor.

Some people don't like this kind of talk. They think we should be harder on others. They think diving for underwater treasure isn't worth it. They think it's better to come crashing down on people with constant corrections. Well, they're free to have their own opinions, and maybe that's the way to go for drill sergeants and parents with teenagers. (Yes, parents, I'm kidding.) But our emphasis here is on mercy, and it includes the merciful outlook as part of the program. Nevertheless, while these reflections are for little souls, we're definitely not taking the soft approach that sees no evil. The merciful outlook doesn't pretend that sin and annoyances aren't there. They're there. We all know they're there. The merciful outlook just makes a strategic choice to go past them. It makes a strategic choice to go for what St. Ignatius would call "the greater good." It chooses mercy over justice and trusts in the power of mercy to bring an even greater good out of evil.

While we're on the topic of cynical objections, let's take another one. Some people will complain that all this talk of finding people's treasure and delighting in their good is all too "romantic." They'll say we just need to do our duty, not hurt anyone, and not get too excited. That last part, I think, is the most revealing: Don't get too excited. Now, there's something to this objection. For, if the merciful outlook is exercised imprudently, if the nozzle isn't properly tightened, if our compassion becomes misty, gushy, clingy, and overbearing, then, yes, it's definitely not perfect. But that's to be expected. Loving is messy business, and it takes time to get it right.

Actually, it's not business at all. It's art. And great artists begin by making mistakes. Even Michelangelo must have started out with his share of messy canvases and broken statues, but God bless the one who tries! For loving is everything, and God is pleased with the person who doesn't lose heart after embarrassing himself trying to love. He's so happy when we don't give up after learning firsthand what it means to be a "fool for Christ's sake" (1 Cor 4:10).

Yet how many people — people who had such beautiful, loving, and compassionate hearts! — have already given up? How many people, after feeling embarrassed, foolish, or hurt because their love came out messy or was misunderstood, have then said to themselves, "That's the last time I'm opening up"? How many people close up their hearts and decide to take the safe route of "not getting too excited"? Cynicism and hardness of heart are not signs of prudence. They're signs of quitting, cowardice, buried talents, and hidden light. But Jesus doesn't want our light hidden. He wants it shining for all to see (see Mt 5:14-16), and even if we burn down a few fields on our way to the lampstand, there's no need to worry — they'll grow back.

One last cynical objection (cynicism dies hard):

> Yeah, that's just great. Set people up for a big fall. Lift those ideals so high that when people come crashing back down to reality, the impact's sure to break their necks (and hearts) — because that's what's going to happen. They'll climb up that high lampstand, find out their lamp was never even lit, and then jump off in despair.

There's something to this objection, too. The merciful outlook ideal is definitely high: to delight in each person we meet. That's not easy. It's not easy to delight in the people we see every day. It's not easy to find treasure in people day in and day out, especially when there's a lot going on. It's not easy, and we often don't do it. Of course we'll fail — but we'll also succeed, and the successes are worth the pain of failure. So, yes, to the extent that our duties allow us, we should try to reach our ideal. It's not possible to live perfectly, but it is possible to live. Why? Because people really do have an amazing beauty that comes from being the unique members of the Body of Christ they are (or are called to be). Even if we see them every day for the rest of our lives, there's no exhausting their richness.

But how do we know this? How do we know all that beauty is really there? After all, most of the time it might seem like it's not there. People are people — and, frankly, we do seem to be a motley crew. Moreover, the day-in, day-out people, especially those we live with and love, quickly seem to lose their mystery.

One test shows that each person is an inexhaustible beauty: death. Someone we know and love suddenly dies. Just as suddenly, the person is not so mundane. Suddenly, we easily see past his annoying aspects and remember the irreplaceable gift that they were — and, in fact, as we remember them, we often find we love those aspects that annoyed us and wish we could experience them again. When someone we love dies, there's no question of consoling ourselves with the thought, "Oh, don't be so sad, there are plenty of other people in the world." We all intuitively understand why that's so ridiculous. Even though many other people in the world are funnier, better looking, kinder, more athletic — whatever — none of that matters. That wasn't the point. There was a treasure in the beloved that no one can replace no matter how talented or gifted, and we rightfully mourn the fact that this side of heaven, we'll never encounter it again. We rightfully weep because there's a hole in the cosmos, a reflection of Christ's face that, here, we behold no more.

So, wonder and delight at the beauty of another is something real — we surely feel its absence after someone we love has just died. It's not something too "romantic," though we may indeed be setting ourselves up for disappointment if we expect to feel it all the time. Still, we can try. We can ask for the grace. We can continue to draw close to Christ, especially to the suffering of his Heart, and hope that he'll make our hearts more like his.

The Heart of Christ. Yes, that's the goal. As members of his body, we share his Heart. We can love with his Heart, the Heart that always sees the treasure (and the suffering) of each person, the Heart that always sees his image in another, the pierced Heart that knows at what terrible price the other has been made so beautiful.

Before moving on to the next point, let's review what the merciful outlook is. The merciful outlook is…

> … truly merciful, because it recognizes that mercy is a bilateral reality such that as we give we also receive — thus, it isn't the patronizing outlook;
>
> … evangelization, proclaiming the good news of Christ's love through an authentic love for the other person — thus, it's not the proselytizing outlook;
>
> … a response to existential loneliness that gives a cup of love to help quench our neighbor's thirst as well as our own;
>
> … the gaze of God: It sees the good in others and brings it to light, draws it out — thus, it's not the judgmental outlook, which focuses on and draws out evil;
>
> … wonderful, because of the sense of awe and wonder we feel at seeing the other as an unrepeatable manifestation of Christ's own beauty;
>
> … a terribly loving gaze that says, "You are great," because it sees the true greatness as well as the potential for greatness in the other;
>
> … deep-sea diving: knowing there is buried treasure in the other, a facet of the face of Christ not found in any other, and swimming through murky waters to find it;

... something that takes courage and perseverance because it sometimes meets with misunderstanding, coldness, and rejection;

... to truly delight in each and every person we meet, because we see in each one the unique member of the Body of Christ he is — thus, it's not the over-spiritualized outlook;

... loving others with the Heart of Christ, because each of us is a member of his Body and thus shares the same Heart with him.

2. *Word: The Merciful Question*

Just as there are infinite ways of doing deeds of mercy, so also there are infinite ways to speak a merciful word. Unfortunately, theologians haven't categorized these ways (as they have deeds of mercy). Thus, we'll have to settle for a simple definition and a few examples. A merciful word is anything written or said with the intention of alleviating the suffering of another. For example, a word that aims to give hope to the despairing, tries to get the sad to laugh, attempts to help the fearful to trust in Jesus, or seeks to make the lonely feel less alone is a word of mercy. Here, I'd like to focus on one specific word of mercy. It's actually a question. I call it the "merciful question."

The merciful question goes with the merciful outlook. Recall that the merciful outlook responds to the suffering of another's existential loneliness by expressing delight in him. Well, the merciful question is simply a way of helping us to experience this delight in the other. It does so by inviting the other (by means of a question) to open up, reveal his treasure, and show who he is.

I said earlier that prudence tightens the nozzle of our compassion, so it'll be effective. This also applies to when we want to show compassion through the merciful question. In other words, we need to be prudent in asking the merciful question — it's not a gushing bucket of questions; it's not an interrogation. It's a simple question or two at the right time and place that invites the other to disclose his treasure, so we might delight in him (or, perhaps, even feel sorrow with him). For instance, after small talk and the usual cordialities that help establish trust with another (and if our duties allow us to take the time), we can ask a question about the other's hopes, joys, fears, or sorrows and then simply listen. If the other person wants to share and has the time for it, great. If not, that's fine, too. Simply having asked the merciful question is an act of mercy — but be prepared. Just as a lot of people out there starve to be delighted in, so there are perhaps just as many who long to be listened to.

Because so many people long to be listened to, we can be sure that our merciful questions will meet with responses. Sometimes the responses will be a gently trickling stream. At other times, they'll be like a dam bursting, and we'll get flooded. If that happens, don't worry. As we advance in prudence, we'll learn how and when to lovingly bring things to a close, if need be. Of course, if we're beginners, we just might frequently get flooded. If that happens, don't worry. It gives us practice in learning how to swim through the sometimes messy waters of love, and the next time we'll be able to do better. Speaking of practice, it might be helpful if I relate something of my own experience of learning to ask the merciful question.

For me, the best school for learning to ask the merciful question was the seminary. Several factors made it a particularly good school: There were many seminarians, we had to meet for conversation frequently (at least three times a day during mealtimes), and we were often different in age, temperament, and background. In such an environment, there were lots of opportunities to ask merciful questions, but that's not to say it was easy. It didn't take long for me to discover that the merciful question often needs to take different forms, depending on the person to whom it's addressed.

With some of the guys in the seminary, I learned it's best not to prod. Showing mercy to them usually meant keeping things light, for example, by talking sports or weather and by doing a lot of joking. Interestingly enough, after spending some time on the superficial, they appreciated a merciful question now and then, as long as an injection of humor quickly followed their sharing. Other guys were starving for deeper conversation. They were the ones who felt most consoled by any question that asked about their joys and sorrows, hopes and fears. They were also the ones who gave me the most practice in learning to lovingly manage floods. Then there were the intellectuals who were eager to delve into questions of philosophy or the mysteries of faith. With them, the merciful question was easy. I'd simply ask, "So, what'd you learn in class today?" Then it would begin. Once we got into it, and I was asked my opinion, I have to confess that I was usually the one responsible for doing the flooding (especially if the topic was Divine Mercy or Ignatian spirituality), which brings me to one last point about the merciful question.

We ourselves should be open to answering the merciful questions others pose to us. Once again, as St. Pope John Paul II wrote, mercy is a bilateral reality. Thus, while the one who shares receives the gift of being listened to, there's also a gift for the person who gets to listen, who gets to see the treasure of the other open up. We all have inner riches, and we shouldn't be afraid to share them with others. However, we might want to make sure that the other really is open (maybe their question was just small talk), and we might want to strive not to flood them. If we're not sure how open the other is, before we begin, it doesn't hurt to ask something like, "Well, how much time do you have?" If we end up flooding them anyway, at least we're giving them an opportunity to learn to swim, and we can make a mental note to do better the next time.

3. Prayer: The Prayers of Mercy

The third degree of mercy, "Prayer," was covered earlier on pages 96-111. For a list of specific mercy prayers, see Appendix Two, which now follows.

APPENDIX TWO

Mercy Prayers and Meditations

Contents

CHAPLET OF DIVINE MERCY
(*Diary*, 475-476)

The Chaplet of Divine Mercy is recited using ordinary rosary beads of five decades. The chaplet is usually preceded by an optional opening prayer from the *Diary of Saint Faustina* (1319, 84), followed by a closing prayer (446), and a second closing prayer that is recommended (950).

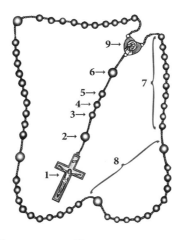

(1) MAKE THE SIGN OF THE CROSS
In the name of the Father, and of the Son, and of the Holy Spirit. Amen.

(2) OPTIONAL OPENING PRAYER
You expired, Jesus, but the source of life gushed forth for souls, and the ocean of mercy opened up for the whole world. O Fount of Life, unfathomable Divine Mercy, envelop the whole world and empty Yourself out upon us.

O Blood and Water, which gushed forth from the Heart of Jesus as a fountain of Mercy for us, I trust in You. (Repeat this sentence 3 times.)

(3) OUR FATHER
Our Father, who art in heaven, hallowed be Thy name; Thy kingdom come; Thy will be done on earth as it is in heaven. Give us this day our daily bread; and forgive us our trespasses as we forgive those who trespass against us; and lead us not into temptation, but deliver us from evil. Amen.

(4) Hail Mary

Hail Mary, full of grace. The Lord is with thee. Blessed art thou amongst women, and blessed is the fruit of thy womb, Jesus. Holy Mary, Mother of God, pray for us sinners, now and at the hour of our death. Amen.

(5) The Apostle's Creed

I believe in God, the Father almighty, Creator of heaven and earth, and in Jesus Christ, his only Son, our Lord, who was conceived by the Holy Spirit, born of the Virgin Mary, suffered under Pontius Pilate, was crucified, died, and was buried; he descended into hell; on the third day he rose again from the dead; he ascended into heaven, and is seated at the right hand of God the Father almighty; from there he will come to judge the living and the dead. I believe in the Holy Spirit, the holy catholic Church, the communion of saints, the forgiveness of sins, the resurrection of the body, and life everlasting. Amen.

(6) Eternal Father Prayer

Eternal Father, I offer you the Body and Blood, Soul and Divinity of Your Dearly Beloved Son, Our Lord, Jesus Christ, in atonement for our sins and those of the whole world.

(7) On the Ten Small Beads of Each Decade

For the sake of His sorrowful Passion, have mercy on us and on the whole world.

(8) Repeat for the Remaining Decades

Say the "Eternal Father" (6) on the "Our Father" bead and then "For the sake of His sorrowful Passion" (7) on the following "Hail Mary" beads.

(9) Conclude with Holy God Prayer

Holy God, Holy Mighty One, Holy Immortal One, have mercy on us and on the whole world. (Repeat 3 times.)

(10) Optional Closing Prayer

Eternal God, in whom mercy is endless and the treasury of compassion — inexhaustible, look kindly upon us and increase Your mercy in us, that in difficult moments we might not despair nor become despondent, but with great confidence submit ourselves to Your holy will, which is Love and Mercy itself.

DIVINE MERCY NOVENA
(*Diary*, 1209-1229)

FIRST DAY
Today bring to Me
ALL MANKIND, ESPECIALLY ALL SINNERS,

and immerse them in the ocean of My mercy. In this way you will console Me in the bitter grief into which the loss of souls plunges Me.

Most Merciful Jesus, whose very nature it is to have compassion on us and to forgive us, do not look upon our sins but upon our trust which we place in Your infinite goodness. Receive us all into the abode of Your Most Compassionate Heart, and never let us escape from It. We beg this of You by Your love which unites You to the Father and the Holy Spirit.

Eternal Father, turn Your merciful gaze upon all mankind and especially upon poor sinners, all enfolded in the Most Compassionate Heart of Jesus. For the sake of His sorrowful Passion, show us Your mercy, that we may praise the omnipotence of Your mercy forever and ever. Amen.

SECOND DAY
Today bring to Me
THE SOULS OF PRIESTS AND RELIGIOUS,

and immerse them in My unfathomable mercy. It was they who gave Me strength to endure My bitter Passion. Through them as through channels My mercy flows out upon mankind.

Most Merciful Jesus, from whom comes all that is good, increase Your grace in men and women consecrated to Your service,* that they may perform worthy works of mercy; and that all who see them may glorify the Father of Mercy who is in heaven.

Eternal Father, turn Your merciful gaze upon the company of chosen ones in Your vineyard — upon the souls of priests and religious; and endow them with the strength of Your blessing. For the love of the Heart of Your Son in which they are enfolded, impart to them Your power and light, that they may be able to guide others in the way of salvation and with one voice sing praise to Your boundless mercy for ages without end. Amen.

*In the original text, St. Faustina uses the pronoun "us" since she was offering this prayer as a consecrated religious sister. The wording adapted here is intended to make the prayer suitable for universal use.

THIRD DAY

Today bring to Me
ALL DEVOUT AND FAITHFUL SOULS,

and immerse them in the ocean of My mercy. In this way you will console Me in the bitter grief into which the loss of souls plunges Me.

Most Merciful Jesus, from the treasury of Your mercy, You impart Your graces in great abundance to each and all. Receive us into the abode of Your Most Compassionate Heart and never let us escape from It. We beg this grace of You by that most wondrous love for the heavenly Father with which Your Heart burns so fiercely.

Eternal Father, turn Your merciful gaze upon faithful souls, as upon the inheritance of Your Son. For the sake of His sorrowful Passion, grant them Your blessing and surround them with Your constant protection. Thus may they never fail in love or lose the treasure of the holy faith, but rather, with all the hosts of Angels and Saints, may they glorify Your boundless mercy for endless ages. Amen.

FOURTH DAY
Today bring to Me
THOSE WHO DO NOT BELIEVE IN GOD*
AND THOSE WHO DO NOT YET KNOW ME.

I was thinking also of them during My bitter Passion, and their future zeal comforted My Heart. Immerse them in the ocean of My mercy.

Most compassionate Jesus, You are the Light of the whole world. Receive into the abode of Your Most Compassionate Heart the souls of those who do not believe in God and of those who as yet do not know You. Let the rays of Your grace enlighten them that they, too, together with us, may extol Your wonderful mercy; and do not let them escape from the abode which is Your Most Compassionate Heart.

Eternal Father, turn Your merciful gaze upon the souls of those who do not believe in You, and of those who as yet do not know You, but who are enclosed in the Most Compassionate Heart of Jesus. Draw them to the light of the Gospel. These souls do not know what great happiness it is to love You. Grant that they, too, may extol the generosity of Your mercy for endless ages. Amen.

*Our Lord's original words here were "the pagans." Since the pontificate of Pope John XXIII, the Church has seen fit to replace this term with clearer and more appropriate terminology.

FIFTH DAY
Today bring to Me
THE SOULS OF THOSE WHO HAVE
SEPARATED THEMSELVES FROM MY CHURCH,*

and immerse them in the ocean of My mercy. During My bitter Passion they tore at My Body and Heart, that is, My Church. As they return to unity with the Church, My wounds heal and in this way they alleviate My Passion.

Most Merciful Jesus, Goodness Itself, You do not refuse light to those who seek it of You. Receive into the abode of Your Most

Compassionate Heart the souls of those who have separated themselves from Your Church. Draw them by Your light into the unity of the Church, and do not let them escape from the abode of Your Most Compassionate Heart; but bring it about that they, too, come to glorify the generosity of Your mercy.

Eternal Father, turn Your merciful gaze upon the souls of those who have separated themselves from Your Son's Church, who have squandered Your blessings and misused Your graces by obstinately persisting in their errors. Do not look upon their errors, but upon the love of Your own Son and upon His bitter Passion, which He underwent for their sake, since they, too, are enclosed in His Most Compassionate Heart. Bring it about that they also may glorify Your great mercy for endless ages. Amen.

*Our Lord's original words here were "heretics and schismatics," since he spoke to Saint Faustina within the context of her times. As of the Second Vatican Council, Church authorities have seen fit not to use those designations in accordance with the explanation given in the Council's Decree on Ecumenism (n.3). Every pope since the Council has reaffirmed that usage. Saint Faustina herself, her heart always in harmony with the mind of the Church, most certainly would have agreed. When at one time, because of the decisions of her superiors and confessor, she was not able to execute our Lord's inspirations and orders, she declared: "I will follow Your will insofar as You will permit me to do so through Your representative. O my Jesus, I give priority to the voice of the Church over the voice with which You speak to me" (*Diary*, 497). The Lord confirmed her action and praised her for it.

SIXTH DAY
Today bring to Me
THE MEEK AND HUMBLE SOULS
AND THE SOULS OF LITTLE CHILDREN,

and immerse them in My mercy. These souls most closely resemble My Heart. They strengthened Me during My bitter agony. I saw them as earthly Angels, who will keep vigil at My altars. I pour out upon them whole torrents of grace. Only the humble soul is capable of receiving My grace. I favor humble souls with My confidence.

Most Merciful Jesus, You Yourself have said, "Learn from Me for I am meek and humble of heart." Receive into the abode of Your Most Compassionate Heart all meek and humble souls and the souls of little children. These souls send all heaven into ecstasy and they are the heavenly Father's favorites. They are a sweet-smelling bouquet before the throne of God; God Himself takes delight in their fragrance. These souls have a permanent abode in Your Most Compassionate Heart, O Jesus, and they unceasingly sing out a hymn of love and mercy.

Eternal Father, turn Your merciful gaze upon meek souls, upon humble souls, and upon little children who are enfolded in the abode which is the Most Compassionate Heart of Jesus. These souls bear the closest resemblance to Your Son. Their fragrance rises from the earth and reaches Your very throne. Father of mercy and of all goodness, I beg You by the love You bear these souls and by the delight You take in them: Bless the whole world, that all souls together may sing out the praises of Your mercy for endless ages. Amen.

SEVENTH DAY

Today bring to Me
THE SOULS WHO ESPECIALLY VENERATE
AND GLORIFY MY MERCY,*

and immerse them in My mercy. These souls sorrowed most over my Passion and entered most deeply into My spirit. They are living images of My Compassionate Heart. These souls will shine with a special brightness in the next life. Not one of them will go into the fire of hell. I shall particularly defend each one of them at the hour of death.

Most Merciful Jesus, whose Heart is Love Itself, receive into the abode of Your Most Compassionate Heart the souls of those who particularly extol and venerate the greatness of Your mercy. These souls are mighty with the very power of God Himself. In the midst of all afflictions and adversities they go forward, confident of Your mercy; and united to You, O Jesus, they carry all mankind on their shoulders. These souls will not be judged severely, but Your mercy will embrace them as they depart from this life.

Eternal Father, turn Your merciful gaze upon the souls who glorify and venerate Your greatest attribute, that of Your fathomless mercy, and who are enclosed in the Most Compassionate Heart of Jesus. These souls are a living Gospel; their hands are full of deeds of mercy, and their hearts, overflowing with joy, sing a canticle of mercy to You, O Most High! I beg You O God: Show them Your mercy according to the hope and trust they have placed in You. Let there be accomplished in them the promise of Jesus, who said to them that during their life, but especially at the hour of death, the souls who will venerate this fathomless mercy of His, He, Himself, will defend as His glory. Amen.

*The text leads one to conclude that in the first prayer directed to Jesus, who is the Redeemer, it is "victim" souls and contemplatives that are being prayed for; those persons, that is, that voluntarily offered themselves to God for the salvation of their neighbor (see Col 1:24; 2 Cor 4:12). This explains their close union with the Savior and the extraordinary efficacy that their invisible activity has for others. In the second prayer, directed to the Father from whom comes "every worthwhile gift and every genuine benefit," we recommend the "active" souls, who promote devotion to Divine Mercy and exercise with it all the other works that lend themselves to the spiritual and material uplifting of their brethren.

EIGHTH DAY
Today bring to Me
THE SOULS WHO ARE DETAINED
IN PURGATORY,

and immerse them in the abyss of My mercy. Let the torrents of My Blood cool down their scorching flames. All these souls are greatly loved by Me. They are making retribution to My justice. It is in your power to bring them relief. Draw all the indulgences from the treasury of My Church and offer them on their behalf. Oh, if you only knew the torments they suffer, you would continually offer for them the alms of the spirit and pay off their debt to My justice.

Most Merciful Jesus, You Yourself have said that You desire mercy; so I bring into the abode of Your Most Compassionate Heart the souls in Purgatory, souls who are very dear to You, and yet, who must make retribution to Your justice. May the streams of Blood and Water which gushed forth from Your Heart put out the flames of Purgatory, that there, too, the power of Your mercy may be celebrated.

Eternal Father, turn Your merciful gaze upon the souls suffering in Purgatory, who are enfolded in the Most Compassionate Heart of Jesus. I beg You, by the sorrowful Passion of Jesus Your Son, and by all the bitterness with which His most sacred Soul was flooded: Manifest Your mercy to the souls who are under Your just scrutiny. Look upon them in no other way but only through the Wounds of Jesus, Your dearly beloved Son; for we firmly believe that there is no limit to Your goodness and compassion. Amen.

NINTH DAY

**Today bring to Me
SOULS WHO HAVE BECOME LUKEWARM,***

and immerse them in the abyss of My mercy. These souls wound My Heart most painfully. My soul suffered the most dreadful loathing in the Garden of Olives because of lukewarm souls. They were the reason I cried out: "Father, take this cup away from Me, if it be Your will." For them, the last hope of salvation is to run to My mercy.

Most compassionate Jesus, You are Compassion Itself. I bring lukewarm souls into the abode of Your Most Compassionate Heart. In this fire of Your pure love, let these tepid souls, who, like corpses, filled You with such deep loathing, be once again set aflame. O Most Compassionate Jesus, exercise the omnipotence of Your mercy and draw them into the very ardor of Your love, and bestow upon them the gift of holy love, for nothing is beyond Your power.

Eternal Father, turn Your merciful gaze upon lukewarm souls who are nonetheless enfolded in the Most Compassionate

Heart of Jesus. Father of Mercy, I beg You by the bitter Passion of Your Son and by His three-hour agony on the Cross: Let them, too, glorify the abyss of Your mercy. Amen.

*To understand who are the souls designated for this day, and who in the *Diary* are called "lukewarm," but are also compared to ice and to corpses, we would do well to take note of the definition that the Savior himself gave to them when speaking to St. Faustina about them on one occasion: **There are souls who thwart My efforts** (1682). **Souls without love or devotion, souls full of egoism and selfishness, proud and arrogant souls full of deceit and hypocrisy, lukewarm souls who have just enough warmth to keep themselves alive: My Heart cannot bear this. All the graces that I pour out upon them flow off them as off the face of a rock. I cannot stand them because they are neither good nor bad** (1702).

LITANY OF DIVINE MERCY
(*Diary*, 948-49)

Divine Mercy, gushing forth from the bosom of the Father,
  I Trust in You.
Divine Mercy, greatest attribute of God,
  I Trust in You.
Divine Mercy, incomprehensible mystery,
  I Trust in You.
Divine Mercy, fountain gushing forth from the mystery of the Most Blessed Trinity,
  I Trust in You.
Divine Mercy, unfathomed by any intellect, human or angelic,
  I Trust in You.
Divine Mercy, from which wells forth all life and happiness,
  I Trust in You.
Divine Mercy, better than the heavens,
  I Trust in You.
Divine Mercy, source of miracles and wonders,
  I Trust in You.
Divine Mercy, encompassing the whole universe,
  I Trust in You.
Divine Mercy, descending to earth in the Person of the Incarnate Word,
  I Trust in You.

Divine Mercy, which flowed out from the open wound of the Heart of Jesus,
> *I Trust in You.*

Divine Mercy, enclosed in the Heart of Jesus for us, and especially for sinners,
> *I Trust in You.*

Divine Mercy, unfathomed in the institution of the Sacred Host,
> *I Trust in You.*

Divine Mercy, in the founding of Holy Church,
> *I Trust in You.*

Divine Mercy, in the Sacrament of Holy Baptism,
> *I Trust in You.*

Divine Mercy, in our justification through Jesus Christ,
> *I Trust in You.*

Divine Mercy, accompanying us through our whole life,
> *I Trust in You.*

Divine Mercy, embracing us especially at the hour of death,
> *I Trust in You.*

Divine Mercy, endowing us with immortal life,
> *I Trust in You.*

Divine Mercy, accompanying us every moment of our life,
> *I Trust in You.*

Divine Mercy, shielding us from the fire of hell,
> *I Trust in You.*

Divine Mercy, in the conversion of hardened sinners,
> *I Trust in You.*

Divine Mercy, astonishment for Angels, incomprehensible to Saints,
> *I Trust in You.*

Divine Mercy, unfathomed in all the mysteries of God,
> *I Trust in You.*

Divine Mercy, lifting us out of every misery,
> *I Trust in You.*

Divine Mercy, source of our happiness and joy,
> *I Trust in You.*

Divine Mercy, in calling us forth from nothingness to existence,
> *I Trust in You.*

Divine Mercy, embracing all the works of His hands,
   I Trust in You.
Divine Mercy, crown of all of God's handiwork,
   I Trust in You.
Divine Mercy, in which we are all immersed,
   I Trust in You.
Divine Mercy, sweet relief for anguished hearts,
   I Trust in You.
Divine Mercy, only hope of despairing souls,
   I Trust in You.
Divine Mercy, repose of hearts, peace amidst fear,
   I Trust in You.
Divine Mercy, delight and ecstasy of holy souls,
   I Trust in You.
Divine Mercy, inspiring hope against all hope,
   I Trust in You.

SAINT FAUSTINA'S PRAYERS FOR LIVING MERCY

O Most Holy Trinity! As many times as I breathe, as many times as my heart beats, as many times as my blood pulsates through my body, so many thousand times do I want to glorify Your mercy.

I want to be completely transformed into Your mercy and to be Your living reflection, O Lord. May the greatest of all divine attributes, that of Your unfathomable mercy, pass through my heart and soul to my neighbor.

Help me, O Lord, that my eyes may be merciful, so that I may never suspect or judge from appearances, but look for what is beautiful in my neighbors' souls and come to their rescue.

Help me, that my ears may be merciful, so that I may give heed to my neighbors' needs and not be indifferent to their pains and moanings.

Help me, O Lord, that my tongue may be merciful, so that I should never speak negatively of my neighbor, but have a word of comfort and forgiveness for all.

Help me, O Lord, that my hands may be merciful and filled with good deeds, so that I may do only good to my neighbors and take upon myself the more difficult and toilsome tasks.

Help me, that my feet may be merciful, so that I may hurry to assist my neighbor, overcoming my own fatigue and weariness. My true rest is in the service of my neighbor.

Help me, O Lord, that my heart may be merciful so that I myself may feel all the sufferings of my neighbor. I will refuse my heart to no one. I will be sincere even with those who, I know, will abuse my kindness. And I will lock myself up in the most merciful Heart of Jesus. I will bear my own suffering in silence. May Your mercy, O Lord, rest upon me.

You Yourself command me to exercise the three degrees of mercy. The first: the act of mercy, of whatever kind. The second: the word of mercy — if I cannot carry out a work of mercy, I will assist by my words. The third: prayer — if I cannot show mercy by deeds or words, I can always do so by prayer. My prayer reaches out even there where I cannot reach out physically.

O my Jesus, transform me into Yourself, for you can do all things (163).

My Jesus, make my heart like unto Your merciful Heart. Jesus, help me to go through life doing good to everyone (692).

I ask You to make my heart so big that there will be room in it for the needs of all the souls living on the face of the earth … . O Jesus, make my heart sensitive to all the sufferings of my neighbor, whether of body or of soul. O my Jesus, I know that You act toward us as we act toward our neighbor (695).

O my Jesus, teach me to open the bosom of mercy and love to everyone who asks for it. Jesus … teach me so that all my prayers and deeds may bear the seal of Your mercy (755).

My Jesus, penetrate me through and through so that I might be able to reflect You in my whole life. Divinize me so that my deeds may have supernatural value. Grant that I may have love, compassion and mercy for every soul without exception. O my Jesus, each of Your saints reflects one of Your virtues; I desire to reflect Your compassionate Heart, full of mercy; I want to glorify it. Let Your mercy, O Jesus, be impressed upon my heart and soul like a seal, and this will be my badge in this and the future life. Glorifying Your mercy is the exclusive task of my life (1242).

O God, give me a deeper faith that I may always see in [my neighbor] Your Holy Image which has been engraved in [his] soul (1522).

PRAYERS FOR LIVING MERCY FROM OTHER SOURCES

Prayer of St. Francis

Lord, make me an instrument of Your peace. Where there is hatred, let me sow love; where there is injury, pardon; where there is doubt, faith; where there is despair, hope; where there is darkness, light; where there is sadness, joy.

O, Divine Master, grant that I may not so much seek to be consoled as to console; to be understood as to understand; to be loved as to love; For it is in giving that we receive; it is in pardoning that we are pardoned; it is in dying that we are born again to eternal life.

Radiating Christ
By Blessed John Henry Newman

Dear Jesus, help me to spread Your fragrance everywhere I go.
Flood my soul with Your spirit and life.
Penetrate and possess my whole being so utterly,
That my life may only be a radiance of Yours.

Shine through me, and be so in me
That every soul I come in contact with
May feel Your presence in my soul.
Let them look up and see no longer me, but only Jesus!

Stay with me and then I shall begin to shine as You shine,
So to shine as to be a light to others;
The light, O Jesus, will be all from You;
None of it will be mine;
It will be you, shining on others through me.

Let me thus praise You the way You love best, by shining on those around me.
Let me preach You without preaching, not by words but by my example,
By the catching force of the sympathetic influence of what I do,
The evident fullness of the love my heart bears to You.

MEDITATIONS ON LIVING MERCY FROM THE *DIARY OF ST. FAUSTINA*

My daughter, I desire that your heart be formed after the model of My merciful Heart. You must be completely imbued with My mercy (167).

I received an inner understanding of the great reward that God is preparing for us, not only for our good deeds, but also for our sincere desire to perform them. What a great grace of God this is! (450).

My daughter, if I demand through you that people revere My mercy, you should be the first to distinguish yourself by this confidence in My mercy. I demand from you deeds of mercy, which are to arise out of love for Me. You are to show mercy to your neighbors always and everywhere. You must not shrink from this or try to excuse or absolve yourself from it.

I am giving you three ways of exercising mercy toward your neighbor: the first — by deed, the second — by word, the third — by prayer. In these three degrees is contained the fullness of mercy, and it is an unquestionable proof of love for Me. By this means a soul glorifies and pays reverence to My mercy. Yes, the first Sunday after Easter is the

Feast of Mercy, but there must also be acts of mercy, and I demand the worship of My mercy through the solemn celebration of the Feast and through the veneration of the image which is painted. By means of this image I shall grant many graces to souls. It is to be a reminder of the demands of My mercy, because even the strongest faith is of no avail without works. O my Jesus, You Yourself must help me in everything, because You see how very little I am, and so I depend solely on Your goodness, O God (742).

I shall fight all evil with the weapon of mercy (745).

O my Jesus, you know what efforts are needed to live sincerely and unaffectedly with those from whom our nature flees, or with those who, deliberately or not, have made us suffer. Humanly speaking, this is impossible. At such times more than at others, I try to discover the Lord Jesus in such a person and for this same Jesus, I do everything for such people. In such acts, love is pure, and such practice of love gives the soul endurance and strength. I do not expect anything from creatures, and therefore I am not disappointed. I know that a creature is poor of itself, so what can one expect from it? God is everything for me; I want to evaluate everything according to God's ways (766).

I must always have a heart which is open to receive the sufferings of others, and drown my own sufferings in the Divine Heart so that they would not be noticed on the outside, in so far as possible (792).

My Master, cause my heart never to expect help from anyone, but I will always strive to bring assistance, consolation and all manner of relief to others. My heart is always open to the sufferings of others; and I will not close my heart to the sufferings of others, even though because of this I have been scornfully nicknamed "dump"; that is, [because] everyone dumps his pain into my heart. [To this] I answered that everyone has a place in my heart and I, in return, have a place in the Heart of Jesus. Taunts regarding the law of love will not narrow my heart. My soul is always sensitive on this point, and Jesus alone is the motive for my love of neighbor (871).

There is a woman here who was once one of our students. Naturally, she puts my patience to the test. She comes to see me several times a day. After each of these visits I am tired out, but I see that the Lord Jesus has sent that soul to me. Let everything glorify You, O Lord. Patience gives glory to God (920).

I suffer great pain at the sight of the sufferings of others. All these sufferings are reflected in my heart. I carry their torments in my heart so that it even wears me out physically. I would like all pains to fall upon me so as to bring relief to my neighbor (1039).

We resemble God most when we forgive our neighbors (1148).

The Lord gave me to know how much He desires a soul to distinguish itself by deeds of love. And in spirit I saw how many souls are calling out to us, "Give us God." (1249).

O Jesus, I see so much beauty scattered around me, beauty for which I give You constant thanks. But I see that some souls are like stone, always cold and unfeeling. Even miracles hardly move them. Their eyes are always fixed on their feet, and so they see nothing but themselves (1284).

During meditation, the sister on the kneeler next to mine keeps coughing and clearing her throat, sometimes without a break. It occurred to me once that I might take another place for the time of the meditation, because Mass had already been offered. But then I thought that if I did change my place, the sister would notice this and might feel hurt that I had moved away from her. So I decided to continue in prayer in my usual place, and to offer this act of patience to God. Toward the end of the meditation, my soul was flooded with God's consolation, and this to the limit of what my heart could bear; and the Lord gave me to know that if I had moved away from that sister I would have moved away also from those graces that flowed into my soul (1311).

I understand that mercy is manifold; one can do good always and everywhere and at all times. An ardent love of God sees all around itself constant opportunities to share itself through deed, word and prayer (1313).

[Many souls] **are often worried because they do not have the material means with which to carry out an act of mercy. Yet spiritual mercy, which requires neither permissions nor storehouses, is much more meritorious and is within the grasp of every soul. If a soul does not exercise mercy somehow or other, it will not obtain My mercy on the day of judgment. Oh, if only souls knew how to gather eternal treasure for themselves, they would not be judged, for they would forestall My judgment with their mercy** (1317).

When I hesitate on how to act in some situations, I always ask Love. It advises best (1354).

It should be of no concern to you how anyone else acts; you are to be My living reflection, through love and mercy. I answered, "Lord, but they often take advantage of my goodness." **That makes no difference, My daughter. That is no concern of yours. As for you, be always merciful toward other people, and especially toward sinners** (1446).

Have great love for those who cause you suffering. Do good to those who hate you. I answered, "O my Master, You see very well that I feel no love for them, and that troubles me." Jesus answered, **It is not always within your power to control your feelings. You will recognize that you have love if, after having experienced annoyance and contradiction, you do not lose your peace, but pray for those who have made you suffer and wish them well** (1628).

My daughter, look into My Merciful Heart and reflect its compassion in your own heart and in your deeds, so that you, who proclaim My mercy to the world, may yourself be aflame with it (1688).

Be always merciful as I am merciful. Love everyone out of love for Me, even your greatest enemies, so that My mercy may be fully reflected in your heart (1695).

My daughter, in this meditation, consider the love of neighbor. Is your love for your neighbor guided by My love? Do you pray for your enemies? Do you wish well to those who have, in one way or another, caused you sorrow or offended you?

Know that whatever good you do to any soul, I accept it as if you had done it to Me.

Application: O Jesus, my Love, You know that it has only been for a short while that I have acted toward my neighbor guided solely by Your love. You alone know of my efforts to do this. It comes to me more easily now, but if You Yourself did not kindle that love in my soul, I would not be able to persevere in this. This is due to Your Eucharistic love which daily sets me afire (1768-1769).

My daughter, I desire that your heart be an abiding place of My mercy. I desire that this mercy flow out upon the whole world through your heart. Let no one who approaches you go away without that trust in My mercy which I so ardently desire for souls (1777).

Endnotes

Endnotes

[1] See especially pages 126-140 of *Consoling the Heart of Jesus: A Do-It-Yourself Retreat Inspired by the Spiritual Exercises of St. Ignatius* (Stockbridge: Marian Press, 2010).

[2] This interpretation of Blessed Mother Teresa's call is based on her famous Letter to the Missionaries of Charity family on March 15, 1993, in which she speaks openly for the first time of the mystical experience she received on September 10, 1946, that inspired her to found the Missionaries of Charity.

[3] John Paul II, encyclical letter *Dives in Misericordia*, November 30, 1980, n. 14.

[4] *Diary of St. Maria Faustina Kowalska: Divine Mercy in My Soul* (Stockbridge: Marian Press, 1987), 742.

[5] Ibid., 163.

[6] English translation of the *Catechism of the Catholic Church*: Modifications from the Editio Typica (Washington, D.C./Vatican: United States Catholic Conference, Inc./Libreria Editrice Vaticana, 1997), 2447.

[7] Catherine Doherty, *Dear Father* (Combermere: Madonna House Publications, 2001), p. 16. Emphasis added.

[8] *Diary*, 920.

[9] Ibid., 1311.

[10] Ibid., 1628.

[11] Ibid., 1148.

[12] In 1917, Our Lady of Fatima forewarned us about the present situation regarding immodesty, saying to Blessed Jacinta Marto, "Certain fashions will be introduced that will offend our Lord very much." The "fashions" refer to immodesty in dress, which offends God because it can be an occasion of sin for others. And this isn't a small matter. Our Lady made this point clear when she also revealed, "More souls go to hell for sins of the flesh than for any other reason."

[13] *Diary*, 723.

[14] Ibid., 1578.

[15] See the judgment of the theologian censor on the writings attributed to the Servant of God, Faustina Kowalska in *Sacra Congregatio Pro Causis Sanctorum P.n. 1123 Cracovien. Beatificationis et canonizationis servae dei Faustinae Kowalska Instituti Sororum B.M.V.A Misericordia (1905-1938)*, pp. 429-430. Also, you can find Jesus' actual words where he promises this grace in the *Diary of St. Faustina*, 300, 570, 699.

[16] John Paul II, *Rise, Let Us Be On Our Way* (New York: Warner Books, 2004), p. 75. Emphasis added.

[17] *True Devotion to Mary*, trans. Frederick W. Faber (Rockford, IL: TAN Books, 1985), n. 55. See also nn. 152-168. For some of St. Maximilian Kolbe's words on this topic, see *Aim Higher!: Spiritual and Marian Reflections of St. Maximilian Kolbe*, trans. Dominic Wisz, OFM Conv. (Libertyville, IL: Marytown Press, 2007), p. 15.

[18] Call the Marians' "Gift of Mercy" representative at 1-866-895-3236.

[19] *Diary*, 723.

[20] "World Watch List Country Profiles 2014," *Open Doors*, accessed February 19, 2014, www.tinyurl.com/extremepersecution.

[21] Liturgy of the Hours, Office of Readings, Saturday in the 5th Week of Ordinary Time.

[22] By the way, don't miss the masterful commentary on the Ten Commandments in the *Catechism of the Catholic Church*, 1691-2557.

[23] Fr. Antonio Spadaro, SJ, "A Big Heart Open to God," *America* Magazine, September 30, 2013.

[24] Ibid.

[25] *Diary*, 1521.

[26] Pope Francis, Homily at the parish of St. Anna in the Vatican, Fifth Sunday of Lent, March 17, 2013.

[27] *Diary*, 163.

[28] These Scripture passages don't actually use the word "purgatory," but the reality they describe corresponds to the Catholic understanding of purgatory.

[29] In the following passage, St. Faustina helps us to better understand the power that comes from uniting our prayers to the Sacrifice of the Mass:

> When I immersed myself in prayer and united myself with all the Masses that were being celebrated all over the world at that time, I implored God, for the sake of all these Holy Masses, to have mercy on the world and especially on poor sinners who were dying at that moment. At the same instant, I received an interior answer from God that a thousand souls had received grace through the prayerful mediation I had offered to God (*Diary*, 1783).

[30] Ibid., 811.

[31] Ibid., 687.

[32] Ibid., 754.

[33] Ibid., 848.

[34] Ibid., 1541.

[35] Ibid., 975.

[36] Ibid., 1397.

[37] Ibid., 1777.

[38] The *Catechism*'s treatment of mortal sin falls under the heading, "The Gravity of Sin: Mortal and Venial Sin," and can be found in paragraph numbers 1854-1864. Here is an excerpt from the first two paragraphs:

> Sins are rightly evaluated according to their gravity. The distinction between mortal and venial sin, already evident in Scripture, became part of the tradition of the Church. It is corroborated by human experience.
>
> *Mortal sin* destroys charity in the heart of man by a grave violation of God's law; it turns man away from God, who is his ultimate end and his beatitude, by preferring an inferior good to him. ... *Venial sin* allows charity to subsist,

even though it offends and wounds it (emphasis in original; 1854-1855).

The *Catechism* goes on to speak about the three conditions for committing a mortal sin:

> For a sin to be *mortal,* three conditions must together be met: "Mortal sin is sin whose object is grave matter and which is also committed with full knowledge and deliberate consent" (emphasis in original; 1857).

The first condition, grave matter, is specified by the Ten Commandments. I recommend reading the *Catechism*'s treatment of the Ten Commandments (2052-2557) to get a clear idea of what specific sins are meant as "grave." (Reading this treatment is also a great way to form one's conscience.) Regarding the second and third conditions, full knowledge and deliberate consent, we read the following:

> Mortal sin requires *full knowledge* and *complete consent.* It presupposes knowledge of the sinful character of the act, of its opposition to God's law. It also implies a consent sufficiently deliberate to be personal choice. Feigned ignorance and hardness of heart do not diminish, but rather increase, the voluntary character of sin.
>
> *Unintentional ignorance* can diminish or even remove the imputability of a grave offence. But no one is deemed to be ignorant of the principles of the moral law, which are written in the conscience of every man. The promptings of feelings and passions can also diminish the voluntary and free character of the offense, as can external pressures or pathological disorders (emphasis in original; 1859-1860).

The *Catechism* provides a more concrete explanation of how the "voluntary and free character of the offence" may be diminished when it treats the sin of masturbation, which is "the deliberate stimulation of the genital organs in order to derive sexual pleasure." Masturbatory acts, it says, are "intrinsically and gravely disordered" (2352). Having said that, the *Catechism* then goes on to teach the following:

> To form an equitable judgment about the subjects' moral responsibility and to guide pastoral action, one must take into account the affective immaturity, force of acquired habit, conditions of anxiety, or other psychological or social factors that can lessen, if not even reduce to a minimum, moral culpability.

[39] *Diary,* 1797-1798.
[40] As my friend, Deacon Chris Alar, MIC, explains, "God knows that you would be praying now for your family member who died in 1980,

and because he is outside of time, he can apply the grace of your prayers now for your dying loved one back then." How beautiful is the mercy of God!

[41] Is it worthwhile to pray for people who have committed suicide? Some people think there's no hope for such souls because suicide is a sign of great despair. Well, I say this: Pray for them! There's hope. But don't just take my word for it. The *Catechism* teaches:

> Grave psychological disturbances, anguish, or grave fear of hardship, suffering, or torture can diminish the responsibility of the one committing suicide.
>
> We should not despair of the eternal salvation of persons who have taken their own lives. By ways known to him alone, God can provide the opportunity for salutary repentance. The Church prays for persons who have taken their own lives (2282-2283).

In his book, *The Cross at Ground Zero* (Huntington: Our Sunday Visitor, 2001), Fr. Benedict Groeschel, CFR, drawing from St. Faustina's writings, writes about how God reaches out to people who commit suicide, giving them a chance to accept his mercy:

> We Catholics have been very impressed in recent years by the revelations and mystical experiences of a humble Polish nun, St. Faustina Kowalska, a simple peasant woman who spoke and wrote a great deal about the Divine Mercy. She tells us that Jesus revealed to her that in His Divine Mercy He calls out to every soul in that millionth of a millionth of a second between life and death. He doesn't rely on us clergy. He doesn't rely on the Christians. He Himself calls every soul because He does not will the death of the sinner but wills that the person be saved. He has said: "As I live, says the Lord God, I have no pleasure in the death of the wicked [that is, the sinner], but that the wicked turn from his way and live; turn back, turn back from your evil ways" (Ezekiel 33:11). I take St. Faustina's revelations very seriously, and I have much hope. In Appendix Three of this book there is a passage from her diary in which she records a conversation revealed to her of Christ speaking to a despairing soul (42-43).

For the conversation of Christ speaking to a despairing soul that Fr. Groeschel mentions above, see the *Diary of St. Faustina*, 1486. Two other passages from the *Diary of St. Faustina* seem to apply particularly well to cases of suicide:

> I often communicate with persons who are dying and obtain the Divine Mercy for them. Oh, how great is the goodness

of God, greater than we can understand. There are moments and there are mysteries of the Divine Mercy over which the heavens are astounded. Let our judgment of souls cease, for God's mercy upon them is extraordinary (1684).

I often attend upon the dying and through entreaties obtain for them trust in God's mercy, and I implore God for an abundance of divine grace, which is always victorious. God's mercy sometimes touches the sinner at the last moment in a wondrous and mysterious way. Outwardly, it seems as if everything were lost, but it is not so. The soul, illumined by a ray of God's powerful final grace, turns to God in the last moment with such a power of love that, in an instant, it receives from God forgiveness of sin and punishment, while outwardly it shows no sign either of repentance or of contrition, because souls [at that stage] no longer react to external things. Oh, how beyond comprehension is God's mercy! But — horror! — there are also souls who voluntarily and consciously reject and scorn this grace! Although a person is at the point of death, the merciful God gives the soul that interior vivid moment, so that if the soul is willing, it has the possibility of returning to God. But sometimes, the obduracy in souls is so great that consciously they choose hell; they [thus] make useless all the prayers that other souls offer to God for them and even the efforts of God Himself ... (1698).

[42] *Catechism*, 1030-1032.

[43] *Diary*, 20.

[44] There's actually a tradition in the Church of offering Gregorian Masses, which is a continuous series of 30 Masses in 30 days said for the repose of the soul of a deceased person. Christ is said to have promised to release the soul for whom such a series of Masses is offered.

[45] The suggested offering, determined by the United States Conference of Catholic Bishops, is $10.00 per Mass. The Code of Canon Law states: "The faithful who make an offering so that Mass can be celebrated for their intention, contribute to the good of the Church, and by that offering they share in the Church's concern for the support of its ministers and its activities" (§ 946).

[46] *Catechism*, 1471.

[47] "St. Therese's Little Way — von Balthasar," The Crossroads Initiative, accessed April 8, 2014, www.tinyurl.com/2kwxkj

[48] The promised, special grace of Divine Mercy Sunday is not the same as a plenary indulgence. A plenary indulgence is given through the Church as the minister of redemption and as having the authority of dispensing and applying the treasury of satisfactions of Christ and the saints. The special grace of Divine Mercy Sunday is rather based on the testimony of a saint, St. Faustina, who simply relates a promise given

by the Lord. Unlike a plenary indulgence, this special grace promised by Jesus through the testimony of St. Faustina cannot be applied to the souls in purgatory. However, the Church does grant a plenary indulgence on Divine Mercy Sunday, under the usual conditions, to those who, in any church or chapel, take part in the prayers and devotions held in honor of Divine Mercy or to those who, in the presence of the Blessed Sacrament exposed or reserved in the tabernacle, recite the Our Father and the Creed, adding a devout prayer to the merciful Lord Jesus, for example, "Jesus, I trust in you."
[49] Here is the Prayer Before a Crucifix:

> Look down upon me, good and gentle Jesus, while before your face I humbly kneel, and with burning soul pray and beseech you to fix deep in my heart lively sentiments of faith, hope, and charity, true contrition for my sins, and a firm purpose of amendment, while I contemplate with great love and tender pity your five wounds, pondering over them within me, calling to mind the words which David, your prophet, said of you, my good Jesus: "They have pierced my hands and my feet; they have numbered all my bones" (Ps 21:17-18).

[50] *Catechism*, 2447.
[51] Pope Francis, Lenten Message, released December 26, 2013, n. 2.
[52] See *The 'One Thing' Is Three: How the Most Holy Trinity Explains Everything* (Stockbridge: Marian Press, 2012), pp. 188-190.
[53] John Paul II, Encyclical Letter *The Gospel of Life*, March 25, 1995, n. 5. Emphasis in original.
[54] Ibid., n. 11.
[55] Ibid., n. 12.
[56] Ibid., n. 95.
[57] Ibid., nn. 12, 17.
[58] Ibid., n. 18.
[59] Ibid., n. 28.
[60] Ibid.
[61] Ibid., n. 91.
[62] Ibid., n. 98. Emphasis in original.
[63] *Dives in Misericordia*, n. 14.
[64] Saint Augustine, Confessions, I, I, I: PL 32, 659-661.
[65] Blaise Pascal, *Pensées*, 139.
[66] Ibid.
[67] According to young people who knew him well, Karol Wojtyla (later Pope John Paul II) had the ability to look at people in a way that convinced them of their call to greatness. See George Weigel's book, *Witness to Hope: The Biography of Pope John Paul II* (New York, NY: HarperCollins Publishers, Inc., 1999), p. 108.

Resource Pages

33 Days to Merciful Love
A Do-It-Yourself Retreat in Preparation for Consecration to Divine Mercy

Live the Jubilee Year of Mercy to the full! Get your copy of *33 Days to Merciful Love* by Fr. Michael Gaitley, MIC, the stirring sequel to the international sensation, *33 Days to Morning Glory*. Using the same 33-day preparation format, *33 Days to Merciful Love* journeys with one of the most beloved saints of modern times, St. Thérèse of Lisieux, and concludes with a consecration to Divine Mercy. So whether you want to deepen your love of Divine Mercy or have a devotion to St. Thérèse, *33 Days to Merciful Love* is the book for you. (216 pages.)

Y38-33DML
ebook: **Y38-EB33DML**

33 Days to Morning Glory

Begin an extraordinary 33-day journey to Marian consecration with four spiritual giants: St. Louis de Montfort, St. Maximilian Kolbe, Blessed Mother Teresa of Calcutta, and St. John Paul II. (208 pages.) **Y38-33DAY** ebook: **Y38-EB33DAY**

Consoling the Heart of Jesus

This do-it-yourself retreat combines the *Spiritual Exercises of St. Ignatius* with the teachings of Saints Thérèse of Lisieux, Faustina Kowalska, and Louis de Montfort. (428 pages.) Includes more than 200 pages of bonus material.

**Consoling the Heart of Jesus
Prayer Companion**
(126 pages.)

Y38-CHJ

Y38-PCCHJ

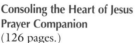

The 'One Thing' Is Three

Learn the key to the Church's wisdom and the greatest mystery of the Catholic faith: the Most Holy Trinity. (400 pages.) **Y38-ONE** ebook: **Y38-EBONE**

The Second Greatest Story Ever Told

Father Michael Gaitley, MIC, expounds on the profound connection between Divine Mercy and Marian consecration, culminating in the person of John Paul II. A must-read for all those who desire to bear witness to the mercy of God. (240 pages.) **Y38-SGSBK** ebook: **Y38-EBSGSBK**

Divine Mercy in the Second Greatest Story (DVD and Guidebook)

NEW!

Exciting 10-part series with DVD and workbook hosted and written by Fr. Michael Gaitley and based on his bestselling book *The Second Greatest Story Ever Told.*

Y38-SGBK

Y38-SGDVD

For our complete line of books, prayercards, pamphlets, and more, visit ShopMercy.org or call 1-800-462-7426.

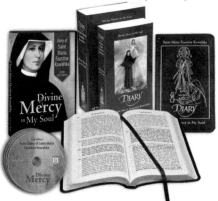

Hearts Afire: Parish-based Programs
from the Marian Fathers of the Immaculate Conception (HAPP®)

STAGE ONE: The Two Hearts

PART 1:
The Immaculate Heart

We begin our journey to the Immaculate Heart with the book *33 Days to Morning Glory* and its accompanying group-retreat program.

PART 2:
The Sacred Heart

Mary then leads us to the Sacred Heart, which begins the second part of Stage One with the book *Consoling the Heart of Jesus* and its accompanying group-retreat program.

STAGE TWO:
Wisdom & Works of Mercy

We begin Stage Two with *The 'One Thing' Is Three* and its accompanying group-study program, which gives group members a kind of crash course in Catholic theology. Stage Two concludes with a program for group works of mercy based on '*You Did It to Me.*'

STAGE THREE: Keeping the Hearts Afire

The heart of Stage Three is the **Marian Missionaries of Divine Mercy**, which invites participants to concretely live everything they've learned in the Hearts Afire program and continue their formation with additional group programs. Become a Marian Missionary: MarianMissionaries.org • 413-944-8500.

Hearts AFIRE
Parish-based Programs from the
Marian Fathers of the Immaculate Conception

HAPP: 1-877-200-4277
Orders: 1-800-462-7426
AllHeartsAfire.org
HAPP@marian.org

Marian Missionaries of Divine Mercy

Level 1
Missionaries who give a year of service.

Level 3
Missionaries who actively serve our mission.

Level 2
Missionaries who support our mission.